THE 400 BLOWS
LOVE AT TWENTY
STOLEN KISSES
BED AND BOARD

Translated by

HELEN G. SCOTT

THE
ADVENTURES OF
Antoine Doinel

Four Screenplays by
FRANÇOIS TRUFFAUT

SIMON AND SCHUSTER   NEW YORK

First U.S. printing

SBN 671-21121-8
Library of Congress Catalog Card Number: 70-185341
Designed by Edith Fowler
Manufactured in the United States of America
by American Book–Stratford Press, Inc.

CONTENTS

INTRODUCTION
WHO IS ANTOINE DOINEL?

A little while ago a French television program, At the Movies, featured an excerpt from Stolen Kisses, played by Delphine Seyrig and Jean-Pierre Léaud.

On the following morning I stepped into a café where I had never been before. The owner came up to me, saying: "I recognize you! I saw you on television yesterday!" Obviously, it was not me he had seen, but Jean-Pierre Léaud in the role of Antoine Doinel; however, since I seldom bother to rectify a misunderstanding, I let this one go and simply asked him for a strong cup of coffee. When he brought it over, he took a closer look at me and added: "That film must have been made a long time ago. You looked much younger then!"

The reason I mention this incident is that it illustrates fairly well the ambiguity (as well as the ubiquity) of that imaginary personage, Antoine Doinel, who happens to be the synthesis of two real-life people: Jean-Pierre Léaud and myself.

I might also quote the news dealer on the Rue Marbeuf, who said to me a few days ago: "Your son came by this morning."

"My son?"

"Yes, the young actor!"

In September 1958 I advertised in France-Soir for a thirteen-year-old youngster to play the leading role in The 400 Blows. Some sixty boys showed up and we did some 16-millimeter tests of each of them. I simply asked them a few easy questions, for what I was hoping to find was a moral resemblance to the child I thought I had been rather than a physical one.

Many of the boys had responded to the ad out of simple curiosity, or at the insistence of their parents. Jean-Pierre Léaud was different: he desperately wanted that role, and though he was thoroughly intimidated, he did his best to appear cheerful and relaxed. This initial encounter left me with the feeling that he was very tense and anxiety-ridden.

On the following week we made some more tests; once again Jean-Pierre Léaud made the most vivid impression of the group. I decided to cast him in the role of Antoine Doinel. The rest of the boys were used in the many classroom scenes throughout the picture.

At the age of fourteen, Jean-Pierre Léaud was not as secretive as is Antoine Doinel, who is furtive in everything he does and pretends to be submissive but in reality does exactly as he pleases.

Like Doinel, Jean-Pierre was an antisocial loner and on the brink of rebellion; however, he was a more wholesome adolescent and quite often he was downright cocky. During the first test, speaking in front of the camera, he said: "I heard you were looking for a fresh guy, so I came." In contrast with Doinel, he was not much of a reader; while he undoubtedly had an inner life of his own, he was already a child of the audio-visual era: he would sooner steal some Ray Charles records than literary works of the French classics.

When the shooting started, Jean-Pierre turned out to be a valuable collaborator to The 400 Blows. He instinctively found the right gestures, his corrections imparted to the dialogue the ring of truth and I encouraged him to use the words of his own vocabulary. Because the screening room in which we looked at the rushes seated no more than fifteen or twenty persons, Jean-Pierre assumed that the picture would never be shown in a normal theater. When he saw the final cut, Jean-Pierre, who had laughed his way through the shooting, burst into tears: behind this autobiographical chronicle of mine, he recognized the story of his own life.

At the age of fifteen I was arrested for vagrancy and locked up in the Center for Juvenile Delinquency at Villejuif. It was shortly after the war; juvenile delinquency was at its peak and the children's penal institutions were packed to capacity. I experienced at first hand what I show in the picture: the cages in the police station with the prostitutes, the ride in the police van, the criminal-records routine and the prison cells; without going into all the ugly details, I can testify that what I went through was considerably tougher than what is shown in the film.

Having started out with a short subject titled *The Mischief Makers* (*Les Mistons*) I realized that I preferred to work with children than with adults. Initially, *The 400 Blows* was supposed to be a short subject, or perhaps the first sketch of an omnibus film about childhood; we had planned to call it *Antoine's Fugue*. Later on, in working out the story with Marcel Moussy, we decided to develop the story into a feature film. Our main purpose was not to depict adolescence from the usual viewpoint of sentimental nostalgia but, on the contrary, to show it as the painful experience it is.

Adolescence is a specific condition that is recognized as such by educators and sociologists but that was, for a long time, ignored by the immediate family. According to the specialists, the affective weaning, the coming of puberty, the wish for independence and the inferiority complex are characteristic symptoms of this condition. During this stage, a simple disturbance, or upset, can spark off a revolt and this crisis is precisely described as adolescent rebellion: the world is unjust, one must cope with it anyway, and one way to cope is to raise hell. In France this is known as *"faire les quatre cents coups."*

The cruel gap between the universe of adolescents and that of adults is admirably expressed by a sentence in Jean Cocteau's *Les Enfants Terribles*: *"Since the death penalty was not enforced in schools, Dargelos was expelled."* When I was thirteen I was desperately anxious to grow up quickly so that I might finally misbehave with impunity. As I saw it, the life of a child was made up of guilt-bearing malfeasances, whereas adult offenses were regarded as simple accidents. If I happened to break a plate while doing the dishes, I would steal down the stairs and furtively throw the pieces in the sewer; that very evening I would hear some friends of my parents laughingly tell of how they had smashed their car against a tree.

I have never changed my mind on that point, and even today, when I hear an adult reminiscing regretfully about his childhood, I tend to think that he has a very poor memory.

I had often thought of filming a sequel to *The 400 Blows* but feared it might be taken as the exploitation of a "good thing." Later on I regretted giving way to that fear, so in 1962, when I was asked to contribute a French sketch to an international omnibus film titled *Love at Twenty*, I took advantage of the opportunity to bring Antoine Doinel back to the screen. In the sketch, titled "Antoine and Colette," we see Antoine's first love affair: he falls in love with a girl he's met at a concert for young people, tries to get close to her and moves to a little hotel right across the street from where she lives with her family. He winds up becoming very friendly with the parents, but losing the girl! It is a cruel story, but I handled it in a light vein. Here again I transposed some personal memories, replacing the passion for cinema by a passion for music, and the moviegoing by concertgoing. All parents have noticed that their children are invariably reluctant to read the books they press upon them: "Read this book. It was my favorite when I was your age." This explains Antoine's failure in *Love at Twenty*: Colette has no use at all for a boy who appeals to her parents!

In *Stolen Kisses*, which I made in 1968, we meet Antoine Doinel five years later, just getting out of the Army and trying to adjust to civilian life. These new adventures were conceived and written together with my friends Claude de Givray and Bernard Revon. We decided that Antoine Doinel would work at several different jobs that would lead him into a variety of situations; at the same time, we didn't want our picture to be a sketch film. Finally, we found our solution on the back cover of a telephone directory, in the form of an ad: "Dubly Agency. Private Investigations." The métier of private detective, unlike that of a secret agent, is true to life; it would provide the ideal context for the many ideas we had in mind. For fantasy is more acceptable to the audience when it is rooted in realism, and "reality," according to Jean Renoir, "is always magic." With this in mind, Claude de Givray and Bernard Revon went to considerable trouble to look up authentic details in various hotels, repair services, shoe stores, garages and particularly at the Dubly Agency, which provided us with valuable technical information.

Then we elaborated the story in the form of a loosely written chronicle in which improvisation would have the final word. My two previous films, *Fahrenheit 451* and *The Bride Wore Black*, did not allow for improvisation, since they dealt with abstract ideas. I now felt the need to come back to the concrete, to the familiar occurrences of everyday life.

In a picture like *Stolen Kisses*, characters take precedence over the situations, the decor and the theme; the characters are more important than the construction, more important than anything else in the picture, which is why everything hinges on the proper choice of the actors. More than ever, I was aware of the need to use actors who were intelligent, even (and especially) when they were to portray characters who were not. I selected the cast of *Stolen Kisses* by doing the rounds of the Paris theaters a few days before the shooting.

But it is around Jean-Pierre Léaud that the whole picture revolves; he is, in fact, its *raison d'être*. If the audience expected *Stolen Kisses* to be a statement of modern youth, they were bound to be disappointed, for it is precisely because of his anachronism and romanticism that I found Jean-Pierre so appealing: he is a young man of the nineteenth century. As for myself, I am a nostalgic; I am not tuned in on what is modern, it is in the past that I find my inspiration; I proceed by personal sensations, which is why all my pictures, and especially *Stolen Kisses*, are filled with souvenirs and tend to remind the audience that sees them of its own youth.

Once a picture is finished I realize it is sadder than I meant it to be. This happens with every picture. I had expected *Stolen Kisses* to be a funny picture. When I started making movies I had the idea that there were things that were funny and others that were sad, so I would put funny things and sad things in my films. Then I tried to switch abruptly from something sad to something comical. In the course of making *Stolen Kisses* I came to feel that the best of all were the kind of situations that were funny and sad at once.

Stolen Kisses was dedicated to Henri Langlois for it was filmed while what has come to be known as "L'Affaire de la Cinémathèque" was taking place, with the French government trying to take over a stock of films that Langlois had accumulated over a thirty-year period. I started shooting on February 5, 1968. On the ninth, having attended a board meeting of the Cinémathèque Française at which Henri Langlois was ousted by a governmental vote and replaced by one Pierre Barbin, I turned up on the set two hours late. From that time on I led a double life as a film maker and a militant agitator, making phone calls between takes to raise funds, alert public opinion, set up a Defense Committee and frequently missing rushes to attend demonstrations. Throughout the shooting our slogan was: "If *Stolen Kisses* is good, it will be thanks to Langlois; if it's bad, we'll blame it on Barbin!"

Eventually, Henri Langlois was reinstated, *Stolen Kisses* was completed, and the première was, of course, held at the Cinémathèque. Afterward, Langlois told me: "This time don't keep us waiting; I want to see those two young people married."

I began to jot down my ideas for *Bed and Board* during the shooting of *The Wild Child.* Then I asked Claude de Givray and Bernard Revon to help me write a story on the young couple that, though essentially French, would be in the spirit of the American comedies of Leo McCarey, George Cukor and, of course, Lubitsch, who excels at injecting laughter into the events of everyday life.

It is my feeling that I had a rather severe approach to Antoine Doinel in *Bed and Board;* I looked at him with the same critical eye I had for Pierre Lachenay in *The Soft Skin.* This is probably because in *Bed and Board* we are no longer dealing with an adolescent, but with an adult, and even though Antoine Doinel and Pierre Lachenay resemble me like two brothers, I am never as gentle with adults as I am with adolescents.

Some French critics felt that in *Bed and Board* Antoine Doinel had become a bourgeois. I believe the film itself provides the answer to this objection. In one of the early sequences a former friend from the repair service where Antoine once worked runs into him in the courtyard where he is dyeing flowers and learns that Antoine has married a young violinist. The friend says: "You always did like nice, little middle-class girls" and Antoine replies: "I never looked at it that way. I like girls who've got nice parents. I love parents . . . so long as they're not mine!"

Antoine proceeds in life like an orphan and looks for foster families, but once he has found them, he tends to run away, for he remains by nature an escapist. Doinel does not openly oppose society (and in this sense he is not a revolutionary), but he is wary of it and goes his own way, on the outskirts of society. He looks for acceptance by those he loves and admires, for his good will is unconditional. Antoine Doinel is far from being an exemplary character: he has charm and takes advantage of it, he lies a great deal and demands more love than he is willing to offer; he is not man in general, he is a man in particular. Antoine Doinel loves life; he especially loves no longer being a child—that is, someone who has no say about what he does, someone who is left aside, who is either overlooked or brutally rejected.

Where did I find the name of Antoine Doinel? For a long time I thought I had made it up, until one day someone pointed out to me that I had borrowed the name of Jean Renoir's secretary, Ginette Doynel! It was from Jean Renoir that I learned that actors are always more important than the characters they portray, or, to put it in a different way, that we should always sacrifice the abstract for the concrete. It is hardly surprising therefore that from the day we started shooting *The 400 Blows* Antoine Doinel began to move away from me to come closer to Jean-Pierre.

A few months after a picture is finished, the laboratory asks production for permission to destroy all the negative that was not used in the final cut—the doubles, the overtakes that are stored in cans in the depot. Though I readily grant this permission for my other films, I am reluctant to do so for the whole Doinel cycle: I feel as if the film on Jean-Pierre Léaud, freezing him in each different phase of his physical development, is more precious than it is for adult protagonists.

I have said almost everything and, in truth, I've said nothing. I can only add that in my opinion Jean-Pierre Léaud is the best French actor of his generation, and it would be unfair not to mention that, to him, Antoine Doinel is only one of the characters he has played, one of the fingers of his hand, one of the costumes he wears, one of the schools of his childhood.

—FRANÇOIS TRUFFAUT
February 1971

THE 400 BLOWS

(Les Quatre Cents Coups)

THE 400 BLOWS

(Les Quatre Cents Coups)

CAST AND CREDITS

ANTOINE DOINEL	Jean-Pierre Léaud
GILBERTE DOINEL	Claire Maurier
JULIEN DOINEL	Albert Rémy
"LITTLE QUIZ"	Guy Decomble
MONSIEUR BIGEY, RENÉ'S FATHER	
	Georges Flamant
RENÉ	Patrick Auffay

THE CHILDREN: Daniel Couturier, François Nocher, Richard Kanayan, Rénaud Fontanarosa, Michel Girard, Henri Moati, Bernard Abbou, Michael Lesignor, Jean-François Bergouignan.

Special Guest Appearances by
Jeanne Moreau and Jean-Claude Brialy

Original story by	François Truffaut
Adaptation and dialogue by	Marcel Moussy
Directed by	François Truffaut
Photography by	Henri Decae
Music by	Jean Constantin
Production by	Les Films du Carrosse and SEDIF

FIRST TREATMENT*

The figure lying on the couch that blocks the narrow entrance to a tiny apartment suggests that of a sleeping child. In the semi-darkness a few hairs stick out on the pillow. We hear the sound of a door being slammed; a young woman brusquely rouses Antoine from his sleep. Grabbing the bedspread, covers and sheets, she shakes them violently: "Come on, kid, get up, make it snappy." We see Antoine hastily going through the motions of washing, dressing, straightening out the couch, grabbing the milk can and running down the stairs. We see him on the street, still running from one store to another. Soon he is back with the milk, the bread and the newspaper. He opens the door quietly and waits in the foyer while his parents quarrel with each other in their bedroom. From what he hears, he gathers they are talking about him, arguing perhaps about whether they can afford to send him to a boarding school. Hearing the sound of footsteps, he pretends to be busy. His mother walks in, saying: "Oh, you're back?"

* The first draft of The 400 Blows is appreciably different from the finished picture. It includes some scenes that were never filmed; inversely, it lacks other scenes that were conceived later on. It is not so much a résumé of the story as it is a working document that illustrates the creation of a screenplay. The final version of the screenplay does not appear in this volume because it has been published in a separate American edition by Grove Press.

Everyone's in a bad mood as the family bolts down its breakfast. Antoine asks his father for his weekly allowance for the school canteen. He answers: "Speak to your mother." Her protest that she has no more money generates another argument over Antoine between husband and wife. Finally the father hands some money to the boy, saying: "But first I want you to mail this registered letter at the post office." Antoine points out that he is already late for school, to which the father replies: "What about your report card? The same low marks week after week! You just watch your step and we'll make sure you get to school on time." Hasty departure of Antoine, who bolts out the door, on the run, always on the run.

At the corner of the Rue des Martyrs and Avenue Trudaine, Antoine, still running, catches up with his friend René, who is strolling down the street as if he had all the time in the world. To Antoine's "Hurry up, you nut, we're going to be late," René explains that he's cutting classes today. He has a note his mother wrote to the teacher the week before when he was sick; by cutting off the top line he can change the "Monday" dateline into "Tuesday." René talks Antoine into playing hooky for the day. The boys conceal their schoolbags behind the open doorway of a building facing the Medrano circus. "Nobody would look here," he points out. As they walk down the boulevards, Antoine questions René, who's sharper than he is, on the meaning of the word "bastard." René explains that bastards have no fathers: All the kings and even some popes were bastards; that never stopped them from getting ahead in the world. "As a matter of fact," he adds, "they're supposed to be smarter than the other people." Antoine is visibly impressed. In replying to his unspoken thought, René says: "It's very simple to find out. All you've got to do is take a look at your family booklet."*

---

* In France a wedding license is accompanied by a family booklet that serves to register births and deaths.

Early morning, in front of the Cinéac movie house on the Boulevard des Italiens. A crowd of some forty adolescents, including a few girls. Some of them carry their schoolbooks; others smoke cigarettes, which are hastily put out as soon as the doors open.

At noon the two boys emerge, blinking and rubbing their eyes. After studying the pictures of the coming attractions, they cross the boulevard.

Part of their canteen money has already been spent on the movie; they spend some more on a loaf of bread, which they share as they walk along the street (or a square perhaps). René explains how he swipes some of the money his mother gives him for the household errands: "Her change purse is torn, so I hide a bill in the lining; if she notices it's missing, she'll search inside out, and if she finds it, she's got no beef. But if she hands me the purse again a few days later and the bill is still inside the lining, it means she hasn't noticed it was missing and I can swipe it with no risk." At a nearby café the heads of the two boys barely reach over the counter. In a generous mood René calls for two soft drinks and asks for his change in coins. The boys take turns at a pinball machine, with René winning the game.

They head for the carnival show on the boulevard. On a deserted side street they spot Antoine's mother across the way.*

* In the final version, Antoine and René spot Antoine's mother kissing a strange man.

Antoine panics; René conceals him by walking slightly ahead, to his left. When she stops in front of a lingerie shop, René says: "It's okay, she didn't see us," but Antoine is doubtful. "You don't know her," he says. "She spends her days reading detective stories. I bet you she can see our reflection in the window." They run to the corner.

Dissolve to the carnival, with Antoine and René weaving in and out of a crowd of all ages and from all walks of life.

The boys reach the Rotor, a large wooden cylindrical drum in which people, flattened against the side walls, are suspended in mid-air by centrifugal force as the drum whirls around at top speed. It takes guts to try it and René loses his nerve. He will look down from the circular platform above while Antoine ventures in.

Antoine, his hair blowing in the wind, flattened against the sidings, is seen by René standing above. A reverse shot from the viewpoint of Antoine. Whirling around at top speed, he catches an occasional glimpse of René, who seems petrified.

A little while later Antoine emerges, a little shaky and still reeling; he is bolstered by René's admiring comments on his guts. They head back to their neighborhood and pick up their schoolbags behind the door. Before separating, René shows Antoine how he will cut off the top line of his mother's excuse note to the teacher in order to change the dateline from Monday to Tuesday. When Antoine points out that he has no note from his mother, René waves him aside: "Look, you've got a sample of her handwriting; I'll lend you my note till tomorrow morning so that you can copy the wording."

Antoine is home. His mother has left him a list of errands. He gets busy. While setting the table he breaks a plate and throws the pieces into the garbage pail; then, on second thought, he picks them up again to wrap them in a newspaper. Down in the street he throws the package into the sewer.

Antoine's mother walks in. In that irritable way she has with him she checks on whether he's done his chores. Watching her out of the corner of his eyes, the boy tries to figure out whether or not she's noticed him in the street. He is gradually reassured and by the time his father comes home he is quite cheerful.

Antoine eats his dinner in silence. His parents discuss him as if he wasn't there, always referring to him as "the kid." When the father makes a few broad jokes and bawdy suggestions, the boy does not understand, or pretends he's not listening. The parents want to spend a few days in the country and they discuss what to do with "the kid." His grandmother won't take him, that's for sure, he gives everybody a pain in the ass, etc. Later on the parents go to the movies; the kid is instructed to go right to bed as soon as he's finished the dishes. Is that clear?

After the parents leave, Antoine rushes through his chores, wiping several dishes at once; he cleans out the sink, spreads out the dish towels to dry. With the feverish haste we have already seen, he rushes down the stairs to empty the garbage, runs up again, looks for the family booklet and finds it. After reading it he looks up thoughtfully. A minute later he's back at work, on the excuse note to the teacher. Painstakingly he begins to copy the note written by René's mother, imitating the handwriting of his own mother. He tears up several sheets of writing because of a spot or a spelling mistake, and once because he has written down René's name instead of his own. Finally, discouraged by his shaky handwriting and not a little frightened, he gives up as the sound of footsteps is heard on the stairs. He pushes his couch aside to clear the doorway a little and goes to bed. As the parents walk in, discussing the movie they've just seen, Antoine pretends to be asleep. His mother pushes the couch back against the door. The parents speak even more freely about "the kid."

The following morning the ritual is the same as the day before, except for a subjective distortion by Antoine, perhaps the result of a guilty dream about having played hooky. He wakes up with a start and looks blank when his mother shakes him: "Well, you're taking your sweet time, aren't you. And who's to blame if you're late today?"

In the street, Antoine meets René and gives him back his excuse note, explaining that he couldn't fake his mother's hand-writing. René nods sympathetically and tells Antoine that he can, if need be, go to school without the note: all he's got to do is to invent such a whopper of an excuse that the teacher won't dare to ask for the note. "For instance," he explains, "when my father broke his leg going down the stairs, I had to stay home to run the errands. My mother had no time to write a note and Ducornet didn't ask for one. So think up something like that."

"But if I tell him my father broke his leg, he'll remember he heard that from you."

"That's right, you've got to figure out something better . . ."

While the two boys are talking it over at the lower end of the Rue des Martyrs, Bertrand, one of their schoolmates, spots them. We'll get to know him later.

Antoine decides not to report to school till after lunch, which will give him time to make up an adequate excuse. The two boys go their separate ways.

We leave Antoine to focus on René in the classroom. The teacher is making the roll call. When René's name is called, he says "Present" and hands the teacher his excuse note. "Antoine X? Absent again today." Bertrand, intrigued, looks over to René, who is unaware of his interest.

Back to Antoine, who is gloomily wandering around. At noon he is alarmed when he fails to find his schoolbag behind the door-way. (By mistake, he's looked behind the left side of the door instead of the right side, where he put it.)

At 12:30 P.M. we see Bertrand going to Antoine's house: "I've come to find out whether Antoine is sick. He hasn't been to school for the past two days." The dumfounded parents exchange meaningful looks.

At 1:30 Antoine reports to school ahead of time and goes over to the teacher in the yard. Looking pale and drawn, he plunges into his monumental lie: "It's my father, you see . . ."

The teacher, with a skeptical look, says: "What about your father?" and Antoine blurts out: "He's dead."

"My God! Excuse me, son, I had no idea . . ."

The whistle blows, summoning the boys into the classroom. René walks over to Antoine: "Did it work?"

"Yes."

"What sort of excuse did you come up with?"

"Leave me alone!"

In the classroom the teacher is visibly moved. Antoine is on his best behavior: his arms folded above his desk, he seems candid and attentive. "Open your notebooks . . ." etc. . . . Bertrand watches Antoine, then looks over toward René. Behind the glass window, the school director appears; he beckons to the teacher, who joins him outside in the corridor. The boys begin whispering to one another. The heads of the director and the teacher appear and disappear. Close-up on René, who is looking at Antoine. Close-up on Bertrand, also staring at Antoine. We now go to Antoine's POV [point of view]: Not only is he aware that all the boys are watching him expectantly, but the director and the teacher now look in his direction. It is obvious he wishes he could sink into a deep hole.

The director now crooks his finger at Antoine to come out into the corridor; as he walks over to the door, his knees quaking,

the father's face appears behind the windowpanes. The boys have
turned around to watch, all eyes are on the half-open doors. The
father twice slaps Antoine hard across the face and adds, in a
threatening tone of voice: "We'll talk about this later, at home!"
The teacher is clearly outraged at having been taken in as he
and the director look grimly on. The boys seem stunned as Antoine,
mustering all of his dignity and trying to hold back his tears, makes
his way back to his seat. One of the boys pipes up: "Christ! I
wouldn't want to be in his shoes!"

After school René questions Antoine: "What'll you do?"

"I don't know . . . except that I'm not going back to my parents. I'm taking off on my own."

"You're right, but where will you go?"

"During the war, when they were bombing La Chapelle, my mother used to take me down to sleep in some of the subway sta-tions—Jules Joffrin, Pigalle, Porte des Lilas—but I guess that's over."

"Yeah, it's rough."

"You can say that again!"

Antoine goes home to write out a rather solemn note to his parents: he fully understands their position, he is aware of the seriousness of his lie and will no longer be a burden to them. He winds up rather grandly that he intends to go on with his studies. Leaving his key on the letter, he leaves the apartment, simply pulling the door shut behind him. René is waiting downstairs. The two boys go over to his house, where it is Antoine's turn to wait outside. Soon René emerges with a turtle-neck sweater and a package of dates which he hands over to Antoine. René has a solution: "My uncle has a print shop on the Rue du Croissant; the men punch in at five A.M. To one side there's an empty ledge where the floors have caved in under the weight of the machines; it's littered with sacks and debris . . . you can easily hide there."

René leads his friend to the shop, settles him in and hurries home where his parents are expecting him for dinner. We follow Antoine as he wanders through the streets until nightfall. He goes back to the print shop and makes himself comfortable on the ledge.

In the middle of the night he is awakened by the sounds of the workers' footsteps and laughter. Stealthily weaving through the rows of machinery and huge paper rolls, he makes his way out to the street. Pulling his collar up to protect himself from the cold, he instinctively heads for his neighborhood, crossing the deserted Boulevard Montmartre. Near the Folies Bergère, there is an all-night café; there he runs into a young woman trying to catch up with a frightened puppy. Walking slowly and leaning over, she does not even look at the boy as she asks him to help her catch the dog, which, in an erratic course, leads its pursuers from street to street. A young man, emerging from the shadows, steps over to ask Antoine whether the girl is his sister.

"I don't even know her," the boy replies, "I'm just trying to help her catch the dog."

"Is that her dog, or is he lost?"

"I don't know."

Emboldened by this information, the young man hastens forward to offer the woman his help. In a little while he drops all pretense, pushing Antoine out of the way. The boy ignores him, or pretends not to understand. The man now tries a direct approach, saying to the woman: "This dog isn't getting us anywhere; let's drop him and have a drink together." When she ignores his offer, he wearies of the game. In time, Antoine too drops the chase to go off on his own way.

At daybreak he watches from a respectful distance as a milkman delivers a crate of bottles in front of a dairy store. As soon as the delivery truck rumbles off, the boy darts over and grabs a bottle of milk. Hastily replacing the wooden case in front of the store, he conceals the bottle under his jacket and runs off.

In a nearby alley he begins to drink; in his fear of being caught, he bolts down the milk, spilling some of it on his clothes. At the sound of footsteps he darts behind a doorway; as they grow more distant he relaxes. He throws the empty bottle into a nearby sewer, listening attentively to the sound of the shattering glass.

In the early light of morning he steals into a garden on the Place de la Trinité and hastily washes up—a rather perfunctory tribute to the rules of organized society.

For the first time, he reports to school early. In the yard the teacher greets him spitefully: "I bet you got hell last night!"

With dignity, Antoine replies: "Not at all, it all went very well."

The bell signals the boys into the classroom. René, late as usual, catches up to Antoine, whispering: "How did it go?"

"Fine, I'll tell you all about it later."

In mid-class Antoine is summoned to the director's office; his father has come to take him home.

To his surprise his mother greets him with tears. In an unexpected display of affection, she bathes him from head to foot and solicitously puts him to bed. It is 10 o'clock in the morning; he cannot sleep, so, to pass the time, he counts the flowers in the curtain . . .

The following sequence is purely documentary, showing Antoine's life at school and at home.

In school, a model pupil, wearing eyeglasses, hides his homework behind a book to prevent the boy next to him from copying. Revenge swiftly follows: The pupil's prize possession, a pair of water goggles, is snatched from his desk; his classmates pass it around as if it were a football until the teacher catches on. He confiscates the goggles and dishes out an unfair punishment to the model pupil.

Another boy, to pocket the money his parents have given him for the barber, gets one of his classmates to give him a haircut.

The result is a disaster. On another occasion, a seminude pinup, cut out of a movie fan magazine, is circulated from desk to desk. One boy embellishes it with a pair of eyeglasses, another adds a mustache. Eventually the teacher confiscates the picture: "That will cost you one hour after school; those who don't like it will get two hours. And you two idiots over there . . . the same for snickering."

During recess, the boys play games. The one who manages to knock over the five-franc piece balanced against the wall will win it.

On Saturday afternoons there is a course in gymnastics. All the boys loathe the gym teacher. As he leads the formation from the school to the stadium, it slowly disbands, with the boys ducking behind the doorways of the houses along the way. Upon arriving at the stadium, the teacher is stunned to discover that his group of twenty boys has dwindled down to six or seven.

At home Antoine is on his best behavior since his escapade; even so, the atmosphere is often stormy. One evening, after the father has searched everywhere for his *Michelin Guide*, he accuses Antoine of having swiped it. With tears in his eyes, the boy denies it. Convinced by his vehemence, the father concedes it has simply vanished. Later on, at René's house, the two boys are playing with paper darts, using a piece of the brass banister they have swiped off the stairway as a blowpipe. "Hey, hand me the *Michelin Guide*." They strip out the pages of the *Guide* to make up their darts.

Alone at home Antoine is reading Honoré de Balzac's *The Quest for the Absolute*. As he reaches the end of the book, he is visibly moved. From a schoolbook he cuts out Balzac's portrait and tacks it up inside a closet full of odds and ends. He lights a candle, places it in front of the portrait and reverently gazes at his idol. When his parents come home, he hastily shuts the closet door. At dinner the parents are discussing a case involving youthful criminals: "No point in having a trial for boys like that. Send them straight to the guillotine and save the money." The dining room is gradually permeated by a thick cloud of smoke: the candle has set the closet on fire! The unwitting victim of his veneration for Balzac,

Antoine gets hell from his parents, who once again talk about sending him away to boarding school.

In school one morning the atmosphere is tense. A state of cold war exists between the boys and their teacher, who inflicts punishment right and left. "But I did study my homework," Antoine protests, "I swear it—I knew all the answers at home." Condemned to stand in the corner until recess, Antoine is bored and tired; he stares sullenly at the boys who are teasing him. To kill time and show off, he takes his pencil out of his pocket and writes on the wall: "Here, on this date, poor Antoine spent two miserable hours on his feet." After the recess games the boys trail back into the classroom. Their howls of laughter, as they pass the inscription on the wall, are so insistent that they attract the teacher's attention. Enraged, he rushes toward Antoine, grabs the boy's schoolbag, books and notebooks and hurls them all out into the hall, shouting to Antoine that he is expelled for eight days. Antoine takes off.

He and René get together after school. René too is demoralized. His report card is so awful that he hasn't got the nerve to show it to his parents.

The only way out for Antoine, they agree, is to disappear for good.

René's parents are a rather eccentric couple; though they share the same home, they never meet. It's an immense apartment. During the war years, the father made a good deal of money off the Germans; but since the *Epuration*, business is very bad and the nine rooms are almost bare of furnishings.

René's mother spends most of her time in the local bars and his father is away all day. The apartment is therefore an ideal hideaway for Antoine. The two boys spend their evening playing *jaquet*, and one night they get a great kick out of making Ponpon, the cat, so drunk that he staggers off to the kitchen. There are frequent outbursts of laughter and shouts of glee; a real vacation atmosphere prevails.

The following sequence will illustrate certain aspects of childhood. As Antoine and René stroll through the streets of Paris, we see the behavior of boys and girls of different ages.

A little boy is walking along the sidewalk balancing a loaf of bread on his head. Speaking to some other kids, he says: "Look, fellows, like the natives!"

Two boys walking side by side. The first spreads his arms apart to simulate a plane, saying: "Turn on the ignition." The other boy pretends to work the key, with sound effects to match. The first boy soars off into space . . .

To attract attention, René pretends to limp. When they come across a priest wearing a long black robe, they hail him: "Bonjour, madame!" The priest tries to catch up with them.

Naturally, Antoine's parents have reported his disappearance to the local police station. Antoine's father calls on René's parents but finds only his mother, drunk as usual and dressed in the style of the twenties. There follows an exchange between two people who are deaf to each other.

"Your boy is a bad influence over my son!"

"Hah! It's the other way around!"

"You don't know anything about it!"

"And you do, I suppose?"

In any case, René's mother doesn't know where Antoine is, but she affirms: "He's certainly not here!"

As it happens, Antoine and René, concealed on top of a closet, have overheard the whole conversation. After Antoine's father leaves, the mother goes over to the sideboard to take out a bottle of beer, which she drinks straight from the bottle. At the gurgling sound, the two boys cannot control their laughter, but she is too drunk to hear them. Even so, they go to great pains to sneak out of the apartment without being caught; they have to climb down from over the closet, conceal themselves behind the drapes and steal through the empty rooms like shadows. The mother, too besotted to distinguish between her hallucinations and reality, is a little frightened by the sound of their footsteps.

Antoine and René have decided to go to the country; they will will need some money. Antoine suggests they swipe a typewriter from his father's office during the lunch hour.

Since Antoine might be recognized, René will handle everything. Antoine draws up a map of the premises; he will await René in a doorway across the street. The scene takes place on the Rue de Châteaudun.

Everything works out as planned; in a little while René runs across the street, carrying a huge Underwood typewriter in his arms; they don't want to sell it, but they hope to pick up a fourth of its value, i.e., some 15,000 francs, by putting it in hock.

The Mont de Piété pawnshop is located in a little street behind the Gaumont-Palace. In a nearby café René and Antoine negotiate with a suspicious-looking character: they offer him a percentage if he pawns it for them. (Minors have no legal right to pawn anything.) The man agrees and goes off with the goods. René and Antoine watch through the café window, which is just as well, since the man comes out of the shop immediately, still carrying the typewriter, and walks off in the opposite direction. The two boys catch up with him. The man pretends he's forgotten which café they were at; he claims that in any case he was unable to pawn the machine because he didn't have the bill of sale. He's willing to give the typewriter back to them, but wants to be paid for the trouble he went to.

Antoine and René are desperate: having paid for the drinks at the café, they haven't got a sou. Finally when a policeman appears at the corner, the man hastily gives them their typewriter and takes off. Antoine and René do likewise.

Panic set in. Antoine is particularly upset because it occurs to him (perhaps a little late in the day) that his father will guess he has taken the typewriter. René, unnerved by the experience of lifting it, now refuses to take it back. In the heated argument that ensues, each of the boys throws up such absurdities to the other that they wind up laughing at themselves. However, Antoine is determined to restore the machine, which has turned out not only to be infernal but also unsellable. This time René will wait downstairs. After office hours Antoine puts the typewriter back. Relieved, he runs down the stairs and is just about to leave the building when his father collars him.* René, who thought the danger was over,

---

* In the final version, Antoine, wearing a hat to appear grown up, was caught by the night watchman.

emerges from his hiding place. Antoine's father says to him: "Take a good look at your friend. It will be a long time before you see him again!" René is visibly dejected; Antoine is crushed. The father drags him away, holding tightly onto the scarf around the boy's neck; walking up the Rue Blanche, they soon reach the police precinct at Rue Ballu.

Inside the police superintendent's office: "Here, I've just located my son. It seems he's not only a truant but also a thief. If I hadn't found him, he'd still be running." Antoine is led into an adjoining room, where two plain-clothes men are pecking at their typewriters. Automatically, the boys becomes interested in figuring out the makes of the typewriters.

Back in the superintendent's office, Antoine's father is airing his grievances: "I can't figure it out, sir. Some people, I know, are brutal with children, but I never lift my hand to him; neither does his mother. We are not tyrannical parents; we give him full freedom. . . . He hasn't done a lick of work at school for the past year. He's a sneak and a hypocrite; he never confides in us and is constantly conniving behind our backs. We don't want to take him back. Do whatever you want with him; take him away, put him in the country someplace. Who knows, it might do him some good. We can't figure him out. He needs some real punishment" etc. . . .

The superintendent suggests that Antoine be sent to the Observation Center for Juvenile Delinquents: "It's very well organized; there are workshops where they teach the boys to work with wood and metal; they can figure out some suitable orientation for him there. I will charge him with truancy. Leave him here; in a few days you will be summoned to Children's Court . . ."

The father leaves. One of the two detectives questions Antoine and perfunctorily establishes an official report. The boy is then led down to the basement, inside one of the cages. At midnight a station wagon will pick up the boy and his cellmates, one or two Algerians and a few prostitutes.

Exhausted, Antoine falls asleep on the floor, under a bench. A little while later he is awakened by someone calling out his name. He opens his eyes and sees René, who has brought him a sandwich. A cop brings it over to Antoine. René, visibly distressed at seeing his friend in this fix, waves a farewell gesture before leaving. The other prisoners, all adults, question Antoine, who answers while eating his sandwich.

The police van arrives at midnight. Antoine is pushed into one of the compartments, which is locked behind him. Through the wire netting he peers forlornly at Paris-by-night—recognizing such familiar landmarks as the Place Pigalle, the Gare St. Lazare, the

Louvre, the Pont Saint-Michel and the Palais de Justice. The boy is registered into the prison. He is instructed to hand over his shoe-laces, belt and handkerchief. He winds up in a cell where despite the harsh light overhead, he falls sound asleep on the straw mattress.

The following morning there is a brief interrogation; he is escorted through the corridors of the Palais handcuffed to a guard by means of a metal wire with two wooden ends, similar to the contraption that is used to slice butter. He is taken to the Tower for fingerprinting and mug shots. After an almost sleepless night, unwashed and unkempt, he looks like a little convict.

That afternoon he is conveyed to the Observation Center, where he will await "judgment." Crossing Paris in broad daylight this time, the black station wagon heads for the Porte d'Italie.

Life at the Center: Some thirty youngsters are detained here for a variety of crimes ranging from pilfering construction materials to warehouse robberies and bicycle thefts. There are some cases

of ordinary truancy and others of "special" truancy; some of the inmates are boys who have run away from charity homes, etc.

The discipline is based on military rituals: At the sound of a whistle, the boys line up and move in ranks. At night they undress in a room next to the dormitory; the clothes, rolled up, remain in this room, which is locked up. The boys march into the dormitory, where they sleep naked. The windows too are securely locked at night.

A young woman wearing eyeglasses is responsible for the psychiatric dossier of the youthful delinquents. Her title is "Psychologist," but the word is too difficult for some of the boys who refer to her as the "Spychologist." Despite Antoine's reluctance to respond to the tests, she is genuinely interested in him.

"Do you enjoy killing insects?"

"No, they smell bad."

She asks him to draw society, a tree, the family. She informs him that some of the neighbors have come up with information that is unfavorable to his parents, ergo, helpful to Antoine. She urges him to be hopeful, adding that within a year's time he will be able to choose a line of work, live alone, be legally "emancipated," on probation, etc.

After the session his friends question him: "Did she ask you to draw a tree?"

"Yes, I drew an oak tree."

"Well, I drew a pine tree."

"So did I!"

"Me too!"

"Same here!"

The boys all think it's a big joke.

One of the boys in a nearby group has just returned from the Palais; he describes his "judgment," imitating in turn the judge and the lawyers: "The boy's attorney, Monsieur Baugier, had to plead a case in Bordeaux today and there hasn't been much time to study the dossier that was forwarded to me only this morning. Now let's see . . ."

In the dining hall the boys line up in a double file, behind their chairs, until the whistle blows indicating that they can sit down. On each plate is a piece of bread that cannot be touched until the boys are seated. One day a zealous monitor, instead of giving the whistle signal, proceeds to inspect the plates. Upon discovering that Antoine has eaten a piece of his bread, the monitor holds out both hands in front of the boy's face, asking: "Right or left?"

"Left," Antoine answers.

"Good!" says the monitor, who deliberately removes his wristwatch from his left wrist to strike the boy across the face. Staggered by the violent blow, Antoine will finish his meal standing up.

One day of the week is set aside for sports. On one of those days the delinquents cheerfully run over to the stadium. When the match is over, the group heads back to the Center, followed by a black limousine that overtakes and passes them, ducking in and out of a side alley, until one of the boys recognizes his older brother at the wheel of the car and realizes he is about to be rescued. By the time the monitors blow their whistles, it is too late: the kidnaping has been pulled off!

Back at the Center there is hell to pay: the monitors get a tongue-lashing from the director; the children are warned to watch their step and are threatened with solitary detention. The football games are suspended.

The next morning a basement window is accidentally broken; the room is condemned and the window is replaced.

Antoine and two accomplices undertake the laborious job of removing the fresh putty from the window. When the mess-hall whistle sounds, the three rebels break ranks to dart behind a door. As soon as they are alone they leap over to the window, remove it, jump into the garden and over the fence that separates the Center from the insane asylum next door. The whistles sound the alarm. Eventually the monitors, with the help of the male nurses from the insane asylum, recapture two of the boys. Only Antoine escapes. Running faster than ever before, running for his life, he heads toward the ocean.

DESCRIPTION OF
THE CHARACTERS*

ANTOINE'S MOTHER

She is approximately thirty-two years old. The child was born before she was ready for one and she presumably was married after its birth, which accounts for her attitude; it is possible she might have welcomed a child at another time, but Antoine, who was not "wanted," is regarded as a mishap. The likelihood is that she would have married much later on if he had not been born.

High-strung, intolerant, she never lets up on the boy, literally terrifying him. As long as he does nothing and remains silent in a corner, reading a book, there is no problem—she simply ignores him. But the slightest reminder of the childish presence, i.e., an untimely burst of laughter, a question, any noise, a fit of coughing, is sufficient to awaken her hostility against him.

During meals, she will discuss the boy with her husband as if he wasn't there: "We are invited to the Duponts. What do we do with the kid?"

She ignores Antoine's presence so completely that she walks around the apartment wearing only a bra and the briefest of panties;

* Before working out the shooting script, Marcel Moussy, my co-author, and I drew up a description of the leading protagonists in order to clarify our intentions.

in this flimsy attire she gives the boy his instructions for the daily household shopping.

For the record, she is a handsome, sensual woman, who spends much of her time reading thrillers; she is an indifferent housewife.

She considers her husband rather coarse; among the things she holds against him is his way of cleaning his nails while they're eating, his way of treating everything as a joke. She is also resentful that he makes so little money.

On the whole, she is very contemptuous of all mankind and tends to dismiss people with a curt: "They're all idiots!"

She works as a part-time secretary in an office.

Once in a while she unwinds at the prospect of going to bed with her husband. On those rare occasions it is evident that the couple is too young to be burdened by a twelve-year-old child.

Though she is not really intelligent, she is a little more educated than the average; whether she knows what she's talking about or not, she automatically takes an arbitrary stand on any question.

In her make-up, there is a lack of simplicity; she is one more Emma Bovary-in-residence; when her husband refers to her as a savage, she takes it as a compliment.

In talking with anyone she has a nervous way of breaking in

with: "Yes, I see, I see." The truth is that she sees nothing at all.

She is a parlor terrorist, a heretic, on the outskirts of society— the natural revolt of a girl from a bourgeois background who, by becoming an unwed mother, has discovered all too suddenly the injustice of mankind. If by some twist of fate she had met up with a pimp or a swindler, she might easily have wound up a whore or a con woman.

She loathes children in general and infants in particular. When she hears that her cousin is expecting a third child, she says: "I think it's repulsive; they're no better than rabbits!"

She never says "Antoine," but marks her indifference by ad- dressing him as "my boy" or by referring to him as "the kid" or "the boy." On bad days, she's downright sarcastic: "You idiot!"

From childhood on, she has never found a way of being nat- ural; even when she's alone with Antoine or with her husband, she's giving a performance. The actress who plays the mother might therefore appear to be overplaying her coquetry as well as her high- strung manner.

When she goes to visit Antoine at the Center, she will be wearing a hat, which is so unusual that the boy keeps staring at it, and doesn't hear a word she says.

ANTOINE'S FATHER

Had he been in the entertainment field, he would probably
have been a stand-up comedian. He sees only what he wants to
see; he hates complications of any kind and his leitmotiv is: "Let's
not make waves!" He likes to kid around and will come up with a
wisecrack on any occasion. In the morning, when he discovers he
hasn't got a clean shirt to wear, he might grumble something about
"S'no white," but since his wife talks louder than he does, he usu-
ally falls back on irony: "Look, these holes have some socks stuck
to them."

He has a semiprofessional job, but works under a boss; one
senses that his social career has been sacrificed to sports, which
are his hobby. Much of his time is spent at committee meetings.
Behind a bohemian façade, he submits to the hierarchy inside the
sports world, and while he makes fun of politicians, he is not above
maneuvering for such honorary positions as "vice-chairman of the
Paris district" or "managing editor of the monthly bulletin."

A fairly good raconteur, he never spoils a good story by telling
the truth. He refers to his boss as the "monkey" and loves to play
on words. During the family meals, he often makes Antoine laugh,
thereby exasperating his wife. "Ho hum," he might say, "we're
heading for stormy weather, the dishes are rattling," and then sit
back in cowardly silence as his wife bawls out the kid.

Occasionally he allows himself to needle his wife over her
evening dates with a mysterious girl friend. "I'd like to take a look
at that Yvonne!" but he never carries it any further. He is not
especially jealous and will avoid facing up to anything that might
interfere with his peace of mind.

Women are not a major interest: he is twelve times less unfaithful to his wife than she is to him. Though he might speak of
"that living doll with the gorgeous boobs . . ." he prefers to talk
about women than to practice them.

While his wife is something of a snob, he is a simple, straight-forward and gentle man. He cannot stomach feminine illogic and often gets fed up with the absurdity of his wife's reasoning.

He is rather pleased with himself and with his wit and seems unaware that any wisecrack, quoted often enough, loses its punch. He might say something like: "That floozy's a fly-by-night!"

In contrast with his wife, he is a fairly well-adjusted person; a man of common sense and logic, he has a natural ability for simplification. The most balanced element of the household, he serves as a moderator, constantly bringing back to their proper level the many conflicts that divide Antoine and his mother.

Yet, on major occasions—the *Michelin Guide*, Antoine's first attempt to run away, the business with the typewriter—he may display excessive severity (as if by killing two birds with one stone, he was at the same time getting even for the many humiliations inflicted by his wife, his boss, life in general).

While his wife has a bachelor's degree (and might have gone further except for Antoine's birth), he has merely finished high school and followed a few technical courses. Adding to the disparity between the couple is the fact that he is of peasant stock, the provincial husband of a Parisian wife.

In company he tends to show off and play the clown, but in private he is more natural and quite affectionate. One evening, when he and Antoine are having dinner by themselves, he is seen as a very decent guy.

Establish the fact that he is disappointed by Antoine's indifference to sports: "He prefers to spend all his time at the cinema."

Indicate his irritation that Antoine gives his admiration and trust to others than himself, i.e., Balzac's icon portrait and his friend René.

In contrast with his wife, he never reads. When he is angry he will fall back on all the trite old clichés: "If I had said that when I was your age, my father would have killed me. As long as I support you, you'll do as you're told!"

The real nobility of this man is that he is almost oblivious to the fact that Antoine is not his own son.

ANTOINE

Thirteen years old and a true Parisian. From his mother he has inherited an overcritical sense; he is contemptuous of others, looks down on his cruder friends and makes fun of the concierges.

Terrified of his mother, Antoine is at the same time rather proud of her; in a confused sort of way he even admires her. At home he is a real mouse; there is never a peep out of him. But he makes up for it on the outside, where he talks a mile a minute, volunteering an opinion on everything and contradicting people at the drop of a hat. He is not too popular with his classmates, who fear him a little. Servile with his parents, he is arrogant and sarcastic to outsiders.

His precocious pedantry is apt to attract such dubious compliments as: "When he talks, you'd think he was a man of thirty."

Because he is afraid of her, he is cowardly with his mother, but his clumsy flattery and servility only add to her hostility toward him. If there is an argument between the parents, he sides with his mother, who doesn't appreciate his support in the least: "Look, you, just shut up!" But when his father needles his mother, he can't help laughing, which inevitably provokes a tongue-lashing.

From his father he's inherited fits of giddy laughter. Period.

On the verge of revolt, he is already cynical, unscrupulous and tends to be sneaky.

His behavior, when he is on his own, is significant: a mixture of good and bad conduct. He will do the dishes, but in his haste to dry out the dish towel afterward, he burns it. He will haul the coal up from the cellar, but will then wipe his black hands on the curtain, etc.

He conceals money (probably stolen money) behind the furniture; he is constantly working on some form of larceny. When he is home by himself, he imitates his mother in front of the mirror, using her make-up, the eyelash curler, the depilatory pads, etc.

Antoine is also a romantic; in a little while he will fall desperately in love.

His teachers are of two minds about his unruly behavior at school; some regard him as a disturbed child, while others see him as a misfit.

He works his way out of one troublesome situation to fall right into another one, equally hopeless, which explains why he is constantly anxiety-ridden. He is envious of René's independence toward his parents, who, in any case, do not treat him as a child.

Antoine is always beset by money problems: some change he's swiped from the sideboard has to be put back by such and such time, whereas René never has to account for the cash he swipes.

Always late, he is constantly on the run. In contrast with René, Antoine has no luck. If he can go through two weeks of school without being held after hours, his father promises to give him one thousand francs.* A few days later the teacher inflicts the usual punishment over some minor misstep.

Antoine: "On acount of you, I lose one thousand francs."

René: "What do you mean?"

Antoine: "My father told me that if I was held back . . ."

The teacher: "Doinel, I already gave you one hour. If that's not enough, I can give you more. Meanwhile, go and stand behind the closet during recess."

RENÉ BIGEY

He is so different from Antoine that he complements him very well.

He is less aggressive but also far more independent than Antoine and is constantly needling his friend for his servility. He is more resourceful, more relaxed and more Machiavellian.

He is the one who, out of sheer childish cruelty (during An-

* In old French francs, an amount roughly equivalent to two dollars.

toine's first escapade), went over to ask Antoine's parents whether their son was sick.

His first dialogue with Antoine: "I bet you swipe money from your parents."

Antoine: "Me? I . . . No . . ."

René: "Nothing to be ashamed of. I do it too and I bet I do it better than you do!"

René is more "grown-up," less complex, much more ironic, often cynical. René is self-educated and has extensive knowledge in many fields—geography, history, science, medicine and politics. He will speculate on the weight of great men's brains, etc.

René takes all the initiatives. His cruel taunts have made Antoine conscious of his strange relationship with his mother. René's mother, though a little weird, is a kind and affectionate woman.

Antoine's awareness that his mother's attitude toward him is abnormally harsh is what will generate his rebellion.

René handles large amounts of money; he always takes more risks than Antoine does and gets away with it, thanks partly to his mother's eccentricity and to his father's indifference.

René has a predilection for dangerous situations, the thrills of a theft—all the sensations that make Antoine tense, give him deep anxieties marked by stomach cramps, which René kids him about.

We shall avoid the shifting dependency patterned after the relationship between masculine-feminine couples that is featured in most films dealing with a friendship between children, to show that Antoine and René take turns at dominating each other; there is no ambiguity whatever in the relationship between these two boys.

Antoine and René blow hot and cold, but never at the same time, which accounts for their arguments over such "big jobs" as the stolen typewriter.

René tells Antoine all about his cousin, a girl two years older than he is. During their vacation, they slept in an attic: "She wanted to sleep in my bed; I got sore and threw her out. Boy, what a jerk I was . . . I can't stop thinking about her."

It is at René's house that the missing *Michelin Guide* turns up; the boys use it to make darts for their blowpipe.

One Sunday René goes to visit Antoine at the Center, with a bundle of film magazines. He is not allowed to speak to Antoine because he's not a relative; the two boys simply look at each other through a window. He leaves the bundle of magazines; when the guard sees that it isn't food, he simply throws it away.

Emphasize the final handshake between the two boys, when M. Doinel, after collaring Antoine, says: "Take a good look at your friend. It will be a long time before you see him again."

THE SESSION
WITH THE PSYCHOLOGIST

Throughout the shooting of *The 400 Blows*, on which, for reasons of economy, we used a simple guide track, one of my primary concerns was to achieve a maximum of truth and it seemed to me that Jean-Pierre Léaud was not as natural and genuine as he had been in the 16-millimeter tests we had made prior to the shooting.

It was this preoccupation that led to the creation of a scene that the critics later on singled out as one of the highlights of the picture, namely, Antoine's session with the staff psychologist at the juvenile delinquents' detention center.

Initially, Marcel Moussy and I had written a normal psychological session, using the usual Rorschach tests, but at the last minute I changed my mind. A sound camera and a microphone were brought in and I asked the crew to leave the set. Seated across the table from Jean-Pierre, I asked him a series of questions of which he had no advance knowledge, leaving him free to answer as he pleased. This was relatively easy for him since we had almost reached the end of the shooting and he was, by this time, thoroughly acquainted with his character. But even so, he was so spontaneous in his replies that some of them were based upon his own life; at one point, for instance, he tells all about a grandmother who never appears in the film.

In the final cut, we kept his replies, but my voice on the questions was replaced by that of a woman (who is never seen).

Here is the text of the two 16-millimeter tests made prior to the shooting—a short interview of Jean-Pierre Léaud and a spontaneous exchange of dialogue between Jean-Pierre and Patrick Auffay (the boy who was chosen to play his friend René)—as well as the text of Antoine's session with the psychologist, as it appears in the final version of the picture.

INTERVIEW OF JEAN-PIERRE LÉAUD

LÉAUD: I'm fourteen years old.

VOICE (off): You're fourteen!

LÉAUD: Yes.

VOICE (off): That might be a little too old for the role . . .

LÉAUD: I'm not very tall, you know!

VOICE (off): I see . . . you think you could pass for twelve and a half?

LÉAUD: I think . . . Well, I heard you were looking for a fresh guy . . .

VOICE (off): Are you a fresh guy?

LÉAUD: Yes . . . that's why . . . I mean I'm no deep thinker . . . that's not my style . . .

VOICE (off): It isn't?

LÉAUD: No!

VOICE (off): Where do you go to school?

LÉAUD: Well, I'm two hundred kilometers from Paris . . . so to get here . . . yesterday, I took the train . . . I came specially . . .

VOICE (off): You did?

LÉAUD: Like . . . I took time off.

VOICE (off): Are you in boarding school?

LÉAUD: That's right, I live in! I only get out at vacation time!

VOICE (off): So you're missing school. Won't they resent that?

LÉAUD: I guess so, but what's the difference . . . so long as I'm happy.

VOICE (off): I see . . . And your mother's a movie actress?
LÉAUD: Yes, her too . . .
VOICE (off): What's her name?
LÉAUD: Jacqueline Pierreux.
VOICE (off): And you know Monsieur Domarchi, I believe?
LÉAUD: Well . . . I mean . . . I don't know anybody. It's my mother who knows him. Anyway, we bumped into this guy on the Champs Elysées. So my mother says: "Look, Monsieur . . . a friend . . . We saw in the paper that they're looking for some kids to play in a movie." Then she says: "What about my son?" and he says: "All right, tell them I sent him." So after that he sent this letter . . .
VOICE (off): Is Monsieur Domarchi a nice man?
LÉAUD: How do I know? I only saw him for five minutes . . . he's okay, I guess . . . I mean . . . just running into him like that . . .
VOICE (off): Are you generally sad or cheerful?
LÉAUD: Who me? I'm real cheerful, I'm not sad!

DIALOGUE BETWEEN JEAN-PIERRE LÉAUD AND PATRICK AUFFAY

LÉAUD: What're you gonna do when you're grown up?
AUFFAY: Me? I've got no idea.
LÉAUD: No idea at all?
AUFFAY: Not one.
LÉAUD: Do you like movies? Wouldn't you like to go on . . .
AUFFAY: I guess so, but I don't know for sure.
LÉAUD: Gee, I really like it . . . I hope, you know . . .
AUFFAY: You want to be a movie star?

LÉAUD: Well, I'd like to make out because . . . I mean . . . I like it.

AUFFAY: Is that so?

LÉAUD: Yes.

AUFFAY: Well, this is the first time I'm here, so I can't tell.

LÉAUD: Yeah, but you'll see . . . if they take you on, in a few days, you get to know your way around . . . and there are the other actors . . . it's the whole thing . . .

AUFFAY: Sounds good.

LÉAUD: Do they give dramatic courses in the school where you're at?

AUFFAY: Oh, no! No theater . . . nothing at all like that.

LÉAUD: In other words, you just study?

AUFFAY: That's it. That's all.

LÉAUD: In our school we do lots of different things . . . we have a pretty good time . . .

AUFFAY: You do?

LÉAUD: Yeah . . . some nights . . . without telling anybody . . . [he slaps his hands together and whistles] let's go, fellas! We set up a sort of stage and we play something . . . so they're all surprised and we make out pretty well.

AUFFAY: It sounds interesting.

LÉAUD: So for a week the director is a good guy . . . because he's pleased . . . and after that . . . See, our director went to Indochina, so he's always telling us: "You little bastards, look at what you eat. When I was in Indochina, I ate cockroaches" . . . You know, all that stuff . . .

AUFFAY: (laughing): Ours is a hunchback . . . like this . . .

LÉAUD: He's a hunchback?

AUFFAY: Yeah, he's no great shakes.

LÉAUD: Why don't you touch his hump . . . for good luck? [The two boys laugh.]

ANTOINE DOINEL'S SESSION
WITH THE PSYCHOLOGIST

PSYCHOLOGIST: Why did you return the typewriter?

ANTOINE: Well . . . I couldn't sell it . . . I couldn't do anything with it . . . so I got frightened . . . I don't know . . . I returned it . . . I don't know why . . . just like that.

PSYCHOLOGIST: Tell me . . . it seems you stole ten thousand francs from your grandmother.

ANTOINE: She had invited me—it was her birthday—and then, since she's old, she doesn't eat much . . . she saves her money . . . she doesn't need it . . . she'll die soon. So, I knew where she hid it and I swiped some. I knew she wouldn't notice it and she didn't . . . because that day she gave me a beautiful book. Anyway, my mother always went through my pockets, so that night I put my pants on the bed and she must have swiped the dough . . . because the next day I couldn't find it. After that she spoke to me about it and I had to admit that I got it from my grandmother. So then she took away the beautiful book my grandmother gave me. I asked her for it one day because I wanted to read it . . . that's how I found out she had sold it.

PSYCHOLOGIST: Your parents say that you're always lying.

ANTOINE: Well, I lie sometimes, but so what? When I tell them the truth, they don't believe me anyway . . . so I prefer to lie.

PSYCHOLOGIST: Why don't you like your mother?

ANTOINE: Because at first, I was in a foster home; then when they had no more money, they sent me to my grandmother . . . but she got too old and couldn't take care of me, so I went back to my parents. I was already eight years old and I could tell that my mother didn't like me much. She was always bawling me out for nothing . . . for little things . . . So I . . . when there were fights at home . . . I heard that my mother had me when . . .

well, when she wasn't married yet . . . and one time when she had
a fight with my grandmother . . . that's when I found out she
wanted to have an abortion . . . it was only thanks to my grandmother that I was born.

PSYCHOLOGIST: What do you think of your father?

ANTOINE: Oh, he's all right, I guess. But he's a bit of a coward because he knows my mother's unfaithful, but he says nothing so that
there won't be any fights at home . . . he prefers to let it go at
that.

PSYCHOLOGIST: Have you ever been to bed with a girl?

ANTOINE: No, never, but I have friends who have . . . who've
gone . . . so they told me that if I felt like it, I should go to the
Rue Saint-Denis. So I went . . . and I asked some girls there, but
they bawled me out and I was scared and went away. But I kept
trying and once when I was standing in the street, this guy saw
me and he said: "What are you doing here?" He was a North
African . . . so I told him and he said he knew lots of girls. He
said that he knew one who went . . . a young one who went with
. . . young kids and like that. So he took me to the hotel where she
lived . . . only that day she wasn't home. We waited . . . one
hour . . . two hours . . . She didn't come back, so I left.

LOVE AT TWENTY

(L'Amour à Vingt Ans)

(French Sketch: "Antoine and Colette")

LOVE AT TWENTY

(L'Amour à Vingt Ans)

(French Sketch: "Antoine and Colette")

CAST AND CREDITS

ANTOINE DOINEL	Jean-Pierre Léaud
COLETTE	Marie-France Pisier
COLETTE'S MOTHER	Rosy Varte
COLETTE'S STEPFATHER	François Darbon
RENÉ BIGEY	Patrick Auffay
ALBERT TAZZI	Jean-François Adam

Scenario, dialogue and direction by	François Truffaut
Photography by	Raoul Coutard
Music by	Georges Delerue
Production:	Ulysse Productions

The other sketches of this picture were directed by Marcel Ophuls, Renzo Rossellini, Andrzej Wajda and Shintaro Ishihara.

In 1962, at the request of a French producer who wanted me to direct the French sequence of an international sketch film, I decided to create a sequel to *The 400 Blows*, using Antoine Doinel as the central character and René Bigey as a secondary one.

FIRST TREATMENT

It was inevitable that Antoine Doinel would seize the first opportunity to fall desperately in love.

He is now sixteen years old. His mutinous adolescence has landed him in Children's Court. Having run away from the Observation Center for Juvenile Delinquents, he is recaptured five days later and is assigned to another Center, where discipline is stricter. Thanks to the intervention of the staff psychologist, a sympathetic young woman who takes a special interest in his case, his parents are divested of their authority over the boy and Antoine is released on probation.

As our story begins, Antoine has carefully mapped out a solitary and independent existence. He lives in a furnished room on Place Clichy and works as a stock-room boy in a record publishing firm where he makes up labels and files the records accordingly. We must assume that this job is due to the staff psychologist's awareness of the boy's love for classical music. Antoine belongs to an organization of youthful music lovers, the Jeunesses Musicales de France, and never misses its concerts or its conferences. Through his employers he often gets free tickets to other concerts as well.

His only friend is his childhood companion René Bigey, who now works in a stockbroker's office. When they are not discussing hi-fi or stereo, they talk about the girls they knew in the past, know

now, or hope to know in the future. Sometimes they recall various incidents of their former vagrancy, for instance, that hilarious night when Antoine ran away from home and went into hiding in René's house. They had spent the whole night playing *jaquet* and smoking cigars. At one point, René's father, aroused by their outbursts of laughter, had walked into his son's room. Antoine just managed to hide under the bed, but his feet were sticking out. Though the father pretended not to see him, he must have been aware of what was going on.

The following year René's father landed in jail over his mismanagement of an export-import business; the business, which had thrived during the Occupation, had gone from bad to worse since the Liberation and particularly after the *Epuration* period. He was to die in prison.

One Sunday morning, during an all-Berlioz program at the Salle Pleyel, Antoine falls madly in love with a girl in the audience. He will see her again at other concerts organized by the Jeunesses Musicales de France.

Some time later at an all-Russian program (Moussorgsky–Borodin), he works up sufficient nerve to sit down next to her but is too shy to speak to her.

Another day, he arrives at the Salle Pleyel ahead of time. Colette, speaking to a few of her girl friends, gives him a vague nod of recognition. Blushing violently, he takes this as an encouragement to sit down next to her. As it happens, she has simply stopped by to speak to her friends, and when she goes back to her own seat, two rows forward, Antoine doesn't have the nerve to change places.

In his room that night Antoine writes a wildly romantic letter to the unknown girl but tears it up after reading it over the next morning. He composes a simpler letter but can't bring himself to send it to the girl.

Eventually the ice is broken when the girl takes the initiative of borrowing his program notes during a concert. That evening he takes her home.

She lives behind the Boulevard des Batignolles, in a little street near the Hébertot Theater. Her name is Colette Darbon, she is preparing her baccalaureate degree and lives with her Polish mother and her Alsatian stepfather, who owns a garage near the Gare St. Lazare.

Colette's friends—boys and girls—are students like her; the fact that Antoine lives alone and supports himself confers upon him a certain amount of prestige at first—all the more so because he works in the musical field and the firm he works for is very well known in musical circles.

Colette treats Antoine like a "pal." At first he seems unaware of it, or perhaps is willing to let it go at that for the time being. They exchange books and records; they drink coffee or have a lemonade together after the concerts; he walks her home; they linger on the street to talk. It is the familiar euphoric phase of love in bloom.

In a little while Antoine decides to carry things further. On the pretext of returning some borrowed books, he goes to Colette's house. She is not at home, but her Polish mother, a thirty-six-year-old blonde, is very cordial to the boy. Antoine leaves the books for Colette, as well as a rather erratic letter that cumulates (a) an analysis of their relationship, (b) a pessimistic declaration of love, and (c) the announcement that he is breaking off.

Colette diplomatically responds with a letter of her own that is brief, cheerful and noncommittal and contains this sentence: "My mother thought you were very romantic, probably because of your long hair." (Later on, when she knows Antoine better, Colette's mother will say teasingly: "How long are you letting your hair grow?")

Despite his persistence, Antoine isn't seeing Colette as often as before; she seems determined to hold him at arm's length. Whereupon Antoine takes a bold step. He vacates his furnished room to move into a little hotel located just across the street from the apartment where Colette lives with her parents.

René, his long-time confidant, is impressed by Antoine's audacity. He himself has been in love with his cousin for two years but can't make up his mind to speak up. What he objects to is that she wears her hair short.

"I can't really be in love with her because she has short hair, or else I love her despite the short hair. I can't figure out what I feel." In their discussions over their respective girls, each one has a way of starting out: "Well, mine . . ."

Naturally, the window in Antoine's new room looks out on the street. No sooner has he moved in than he takes up a vigil in front of the window. Soon Colette arrives with both her parents. Hailed by Antoine, the three on the street look up in surprise. They go up to visit the room and, after kidding Antoine, invite their new neighbor to join them for dinner.

Days go by. Colette's parents, who enjoy young people and resent her frequent absences, adopt Antoine. They invite him over even when Colette is away.

From his window Antoine watches the coming and going of the girl he is gradually losing. Colette is at the flirtatious age and has little use for a suitor who is too assiduous and far too possessive.

She firmly rejects an exclusive relationship with Antoine and insists on keeping up with her habitual circle of friends of both sexes.

One day Antoine follows her as she is strolling along the boulevards with a young man (the couple do not walk hand in hand, but the young man has his right hand across the back of Colette's neck as they cross the streets). Afterward, Antoine makes a stupid, clumsy scene, which further deteriorates the situation. That evening he calls upon her parents as they are finishing the family meal; he pleads with his eyes for forgiveness, but Colette is going out for the evening and rejects his offer to accompany her.

The only result of Antoine's persistent efforts to get close to his goddess is that Colette has come to look upon him as a member of the family—a sort of remote cousin—and in any case, as an encumbrance to her freedom of action. The story will wind up one fall evening at the Darbon home. The family and Antoine are having their dessert. There is a knock at the door. Colette opens it to welcome Albert Tazzi, one of those mysterious pals of hers who has come to take her to the movies. Laughing together, the young couple walk out, leaving Antoine to watch television with Colette's parents.

FINAL SCREENPLAY

[1]   Place Clichy at 8 A.M. We see the facade of the Gaumont-Palace theater, the big clock and a rather modest little hotel.

[2]   Inside the hotel, a room with the bare minimum of furniture. There are also books, a portable record player, and some record jackets thumbtacked to the walls. On one of the walls, a sketch of Antoine with the collar of his turtleneck sweater pulled over his nose.

Antoine is asleep in bed. Next to him is a round kitchen alarm clock poised on top of a small radio. The alarm rings. A string, attached to the alarm's winder, is connected to a plug that automatically turns on the radio. It is only when the loud sound of the music blares forth that Antoine finally wakes up.

He sleeps in a dirty shirt over his underwear. There are several blankets, which, like the pillow, are worn and soiled.

Stretching, Antoine reaches for a handkerchief under the pillow and blows his nose. From the ashtray he picks out the remains of a cigar, lights it, winces, but goes on puffing. He gets up and opens the curtains. From his window we see the Place Clichy.

[3]   Place Clichy as seen from below. Pan to Antoine jumping onto the rear platform of a moving bus.

[4]   Antoine enters the Philips record-publishing firm and punches in under the time clock.

[5]   A few flashes show Antoine at work as he puts the records into the proper jackets.

[6]   Evening. The employees emerge from the building. René is waiting for Antoine. It is almost night.

[7]   Antoine and René are in a café.

ANTOINE: How's it going on the stock market?

RENÉ: All right. I'm hoping for a raise soon. How about you?
ANTOINE: They're transferring me into the production department
. . . Hey, Shapiro's playing tonight. I've got two seats. You want
to come?
RENÉ: Sure. That reminds me . . . you remember the time you

stashed out at my place and my father walked in? Wow, that room
stank of tobacco!

[8]   Here we have a flashback to a scene that was shot in 1958 for
The 400 Blows but was eliminated from the final version of that
picture. It shows René and Antoine, sprawled out on an immense

bed, smoking cigars and playing a game of *jaquet* together. A noise from an adjoining room in the apartment makes them stop.

RENÉ: Watch it! It's the old man! Here, grab this cover so we can blow some of the smoke away . . . Okay, that's enough.

Antoine hides under the bed. René's father walks into the room.

RENÉ's FATHER: What's going on here? This place reeks of tobacco . . . it's a real honky-tonk! I'm knocking three cigars off your allowance . . . And what the hell is this? Bucephalus is not to be used as a coat rack; he is worth almost a million.* He's a work of art . . . I won't part with him unless I'm really forced to. All right, that's enough. Put out the lights and go to sleep.

[9]   We come back to the café and to the present. Antoine checks the time and looks for a waiter to pay the check.

ANTOINE: Wow! Two steps more and he would have spotted me!
RENÉ: I'm pretty sure he saw your feet sticking out from under the bed, but he didn't want to say anything.
ANTOINE: Where the hell is that waiter?

[10]   The Salle Pleyel is crowded with the youthful audience of the Jeunesses Musicales de France.
    Antoine and René are seated. The concert has just begun with the *Eroica*.
    Reverse shot of the concert hall from Antoine's POV.
    The concert is under way. Shots of the orchestra.
    A series of shots showing the orchestra, the audience, René, Antoine, and the musicians.

* One million old French francs is equal to approximately two thousand dollars.

A searching look from Antoine until his eyes alight on Colette, a young girl who is sitting with her legs crossed. Several looks from Antoine to Colette, who can't see him since he is in back of her.

René notices Antoine looking at the girl.

As the sequence continues, Colette, sensing Antoine staring at her, looks back. She uncrosses her legs.

This scene consists of some forty three-second shots and reverse shots, with the frame growing progressively smaller and then abruptly opening up: it is a musical love at first sight!

As the concert ends, the maestro bows and the audience heads for the exits. Colette is walking out with one of her girl friends; Antoine makes René hurry up so as not to lose her.

[11]   Place des Ternes. Night. Exterior subway station. Colette and her friend go down into the subway. The two boys stop following them and turn back.

ANTOINE: I wonder why I never noticed her before? Christ, I really like her . . . I mean it . . . What about the girl friend? Do you like her? It would be great—and practical too!

RENÉ: You know I'm in love with my cousin. She has gorgeous long hair, that dope, and she's planning to cut it off next week. I'm sure I won't like her anymore with short hair.

ANTOINE: But is she in love with you?

RENÉ: I don't know . . . I haven't told her anything yet. I'm waiting to see the hair. If I still love her with her hair cut off, I'll send her a declaration. I'll mail it to her.

[12]   A title across the screen: "Eight Days Later."

Midday finds Antoine and René seated together in a café. Here begins a series of flashbacks, commented by Antoine and illustrated by the images of concerts.

COMMENTARY: I saw her three times last week. I haven't spoken to her yet, but she's noticed me . . . The first time, it was Tuesday,

they were playing the *Symphonie Fantastique* . . . I was sitting right in back of her, a little to her right. At one point she took her scarf off. I spent the whole evening staring at her hair and the nape of her neck. I couldn't take my eyes off her. That evening I made up my mind to talk to her, and when people were going out, I elbowed my way through the crowd. But she ran into a girl friend, so I followed them for five minutes or so and then I went home.

The second time was on Thursday . . . I got there a half hour ahead of time so that I could sit next to her. When I walked in, the hall was almost empty . . . so I went out into the lobby to smoke a cigarette while people were going in. By the time I came back, the place was almost full. I looked for her and didn't spot her at first . . . she was kneeling on a seat to talk to her girl friend in the row behind . . . When I sat down next to her, she nodded as if she recognized me vaguely. And then—just my luck!—she got up and went back to her own seat. I didn't have the nerve to follow her . . . it would have been too obvious.

The third time was . . . wait . . . it was last night! She was walking along the Boulevard des Batignolles with a shopping bag. I'm almost certain she lives in my neighborhood.

RENÉ: Well, now that the maneuvers are over, it's time to attack!

[13] Salle Pleyel. Once again we are in the concert hall. The orchestra is winding up a musical selection. Applause. In the hall, Antoine is sitting next to Colette. We sense that Antoine is trying to figure out a way to open the conversation but can't find the right words. So, of course, it is Colette who breaks the ice by simply asking to borrow his program notes. Antoine, trying to conceal his elation, complies eagerly; the concert resumes. From a distance we see them whispering together; the man in front turns around as if to make them shut up.

[14] We now see Antoine and Colette walking side by side at night along the Boulevard de Courcelles.

ANTOINE: As a rule, I get off the subway at Rome or at Clichy. How come I haven't seen you before at the concerts? Do you go there often?
COLETTE: Yes, I went to all the Russian music appreciation series—Moussorgsky, Borodin . . . They have them at the Châtelet on Sunday mornings.
ANTOINE: It's too bad we didn't connect sooner, but I guess we were bound to meet in time . . . I believe we live in the same neighbor-

hood. I noticed you one day doing your shopping on the Boulevard des Batignolles.

COLETTE: Probably . . . I live on the Rue Lécluse.

ANTOINE: What do you do in life?

COLETTE: I'm a student. I'm working toward my baccalaureate. What about you?

ANTOINE: I'm in records.

COLETTE: You have a job?

ANTOINE: Yes, I work at Philips. I'm not with my parents anymore, so I earn my own living.

COLETTE: It must be great to be independent that way.

ANTOINE: Well, that depends . . . you see . . .

They arrive in front of her door.

COLETTE: That's my stepfather's car.

ANTOINE: Are you coming on Thursday to hear Gavoty?

COLETTE: I'll try to. In any case, even if I don't go, I'll probably be at the next one . . . or the one after that.

ANTOINE: Fine, but let me have your phone number just in case . . . that way, we can get together again, right?

COLETTE: Right. It's better to call in the evening because I'm not always home . . . Look, I'd better go because I've got to work.

ANTOINE: Okay, good night. I'll be seeing you.

[15] A few flashes to illustrate the following commentary, i.e., Antoine and Colette at the terrace of a café, in front of a record shop, etc.

COMMENTARY: Antoine and Colette meet several times a week. They exchange books and mostly records. They discuss hi-fi over coffee or lemonade. They take turns at walking each other home. Standing in the streets, in front of doorways, they talk endlessly. Though Antoine doesn't quite see it that way, Colette treats him like just another one of her pals. He's either unaware of it, or perhaps he's willing to let it go at that . . . for the time being.

[16]   We see Antoine at the Salle Pleyel where Bernard Gavoty is giving a lecture. Next to Antoine is an empty seat. Antoine keeps on looking over his shoulder toward the rear of the hall. Finally he gets up and walks out just as the speaker is making the opening remarks.

BERNARD GAVOTY: My friends, this is our second session on experimental music. The first lecture was delivered by Pierre Schaeffer. Your attentive silence, as well as the numerous letters I have received about it, reflect the great interest there is in this subject. . . .

[17]   Now we see Antoine stepping into a phone booth to dial a number.

ANTOINE: Hello . . . Colette?
COLETTE: Hello . . . it's me.
ANTOINE: Why weren't you there last night? We had a date. Were you sick?
COLETTE: Well, I said I "might" come. What happened is that I went to a surprise party with some friends . . . real nuts. We carried on like crazy . . . it was really wild . . . but it was just too much. The fact is we fooled around till five in the morning.
ANTOINE: Can I come by this afternoon?
COLETTE: If you want to, but I'm not sure I'll be here . . . there's a chance the whole gang might get together again this afternoon.
ANTOINE: Shall I come over anyway?
COLETTE: If you're willing to take a chance.

Antoine hangs up and seems rather upset as he leaves the phone booth.

[18]   We see Antoine, running up the stairs, carrying a few books. He knocks at the door, then walks over to the window to run his fingers through his hair. The door opens. A handsome woman stands there, looking at Antoine.

ANTOINE: How do you do? I'm a friend of Colette's. I wonder if she's home.
THE MOTHER: No, she's not.
ANTOINE: She lent me a few books and I'm bringing them back.
THE MOTHER: Fine, I'll give them to her.
ANTOINE: There's also a letter for her.
THE MOTHER: All right. I'll give it all to her . . . Aren't you Antoine?
ANTOINE: Yes, I am.

THE MOTHER: I thought so; she told me all about you. Why don't you come in for a few minutes.

Sitting in the dining room is M. Darbon, the second husband of Colette's mother and the girl's stepfather.

THE MOTHER: This is Antoine . . . you know . . . Colette's friend.

THE STEPFATHER: How do you do. You go to school with her, I believe.

THE MOTHER: No, what are you talking about? They met at the Jeunesses Musicales. You know . . . Colette told us all about it. Antoine has a job. You work in records, I believe, isn't that right?

ANTOINE: Yes, that's right. I work for Philips records.

THE STEPFATHER: My wife can raise her daughter as she likes, but I think young people should make their own way early in life. Why, I went to work as a mechanic at the Laborde garage at the age of fifteen. Now, I'm the boss.

He offers the boy a drink.

ANTOINE: No, thanks. I don't drink.

THE STEPFATHER: Education doesn't get you anywhere. Take Victor Hugo, for instance . . .

THE MOTHER: No, please . . . leave him alone . . . don't start on Victor Hugo.

THE STEPFATHER: Victor Hugo denounced evil, but he never told us what to do about it. Don't you agree?

ANTOINE: Probably. Yes . . . well, uh . . . I've got to go. If you'll excuse me . . .

THE MOTHER: Leaving so soon? Colette will be so sorry.

ANTOINE: Yes, me too, but anyway . . . you know . . .

THE MOTHER: Listen, why don't you have dinner with us one of these days? We'll set it up with Colette.

ANTOINE (*courteously walking ahead of Colette's mother, heading for the door*): I beg your pardon, madame . . .

[19]   Antoine, in his room, is listening to a record. A special-delivery letter is slipped under the door. He opens it and Colette's voice is heard as he reads the following.

VOICE OVER: My dear Antoine, your declaration of love was very nicely worded; it reflects a man of experience. Tonight I'm going to listen to Maurice Le Roux. Will you be there? Thanks for the books . . . Oh, I forgot to mention that my mother thought you looked romantic . . . probably because of your long hair. I'll see you tonight, my dear. Colette.

Antoine runs his fingers through his hair.

[20]   Antoine arrives at the floor of Colette's apartment, adjusts his tie and hair before knocking at the door. Nobody home. He goes down the stairs.

[21]   In the street. He emerges from the building. It is Sunday afternoon. He notices a hotel across the street. It gives him an idea. A few minutes later he walks away looking inspired.

[22]   Antoine is moving out of his furnished room. He's piling books together, taking the drawings off the walls. The scene unfolds to the sound of music from a record spinning on the pickup. Carrying all of his possessions, his books strung around his neck, his record player in his hand, he suggests a heavily loaded pack mule as he vacates the premises.

[23]   Musical and visual dissolve. Antoine has settled down in a hotel room directly facing Colette's apartment across the street. He now takes up his vigil at the window. In a little while a car stops in the street and Colette and her parents emerge. The three

exclaim in surprise as they discover Antoine. Exchange of dialogue between Colette's family and Antoine at his window across the street.

THE STEPFATHER: Hey, look at what I see . . .
THE MOTHER: It's Antoine! He's right across the street from our place. Isn't that something!

COLETTE: What's going on?

ANTOINE: I live here . . . since this afternoon!

THE MOTHER: Can we take a look? Come on, let's go and visit his palace.

The three of them come into Antoine's room.

THE MOTHER: Look at that . . . everything's in order. What a wonderful sink. Look, we can see our windows from here.

THE STEPFATHER: Yes . . . those are our two windows. Except that we get the sun on our side.

[24]   The scene dissolves immediately into a family meal at the Darbon apartment, with Colette's parents questioning Antoine.

THE STEPFATHER: Do you still have your parents?

ANTOINE: Yes, but I don't see them very much. We don't get along together, you see.

THE MOTHER: It's a pity. It must be so sad for your mother not to see you.

ANTOINE: You know, it's pretty much my own fault. When I was living with them, I often ran away from home.

THE STEPFATHER: How I wish Colette would do something like that!

COLETTE: You want to bet? What'll you give me . . .

THE MOTHER: Well, I feel that the family . . .

COLETTE: A question: Where is one better off than in the bosom of one's family? The answer: Anywhere!

THE STEPFATHER: Hervé Bazin.

COLETTE: That's right, in *Viper in the Fist.*

THE MOTHER: Colette talks like that, you know, but she really . . .

COLETTE: Shut up and give us something to drink.

THE STEPFATHER: Isn't that something? They have no respect at all nowadays.

The meal winds up in a mood of general hilarity.

[25]   The images that follow show Antoine at his window, watching out for Colette, and the parents, using sign language, urging him to come over for dinner. The scene is covered by a commentary.

COMMENTARY: Colette's parents, who enjoy the company of young people and are rather distressed over their daughter's frequent absences from home, have more or less adopted Antoine. They frequently invite him to join them. From his window Antoine watches Colette's coming and going, although her attitude toward him is exactly what it was before he moved. It is obvious that to her, Antoine's proximity does not, in itself, justify a closer relationship.

[26] Once again Antoine climbs up the stairs that lead to Colette. At his knock she opens the door.

COLETTE: Well, Antoine, how are you? What can I do for you?
ANTOINE: I have two seats for a lecture . . . Gavoty is lecturing on electronic music.
COLETTE: Yes, I know, but I can't make it. I've got to work all afternoon.
ANTOINE: Can we go to the movies?
COLETTE: Frankly, no . . . I can't, I've got to turn in my homework by tomorrow.
ANTOINE: Can we talk for a few minutes?
COLETTE: No, let's make it some other time. Good-bye.

She closes the door on Antoine. He goes down the stairs.

[27] We see Antoine in one of the corridors of the Philips establishment talking with his friend René.

ANTOINE: Well, it doesn't look too good. I was an idiot; I started off on the wrong foot. By rights, I shouldn't be in love with her . . . she talks as if she was one of the boys and treats me like a buddy. Whenever I try to get serious, she thinks I'm funny. Just the same, I spend hours waiting in front of her door, freezing my balls off!
RENÉ: You haven't asked how I'm making out with my cousin, but I'll tell you anyway. She had her hair cut à la Joan of Arc and I love her anyway. I write her lots of letters and they work. Here, look at her answer.

René hands Antoine a letter covered with lipstick, or, more precisely, with the shape of lips imprinted in bright red.

ANTOINE: Fantastic!
RENÉ: And that's not all . . . Here, look at the envelope.

The envelope too bears the same loving signature.

[28]   At Philips. We see Antoine producing a record: the wax, the pressing, the labeling, the trimming off of the edges and the insertion under jacket.

[29] Intermission time at the movies. Antoine offers Colette the record he has just made.

ANTOINE: I'm in a new department. I've been transferred over to production. You want an ice cream??
COLETTE: No, thanks.
ANTOINE: This is the first record I've made. It is yours . . . a present from me.
COLETTE: Oh, that's very nice. Thank you.
ANTOINE: It took me a long time to make it. As a rule the experts can turn out six hundred in one day. First I put on the labels, then I applied the wax. I put it inside the machine and it came out like that . . . it was sticking out on this side, like that. So I put it on to hear what it sounds like for a first record . . .

Antoine is interrupted as the lights fade, casting the theater into darkness. On the screen the Fox Movietone newsreels show images of a ski event in Austria.

Colette raises no objections when Antoine takes her hand. He looks at her, while she stares straight ahead.

The rhythm of this scene is much the same as that of the love-at-first-sight concert. Colette allows herself to be kissed on the cheek but not on the lips. She pulls herself away violently and looks grim. She turns her head to the right and then to the left, clearly irritated by his persistence. Antoine, offended, gets up and walks out.

[30] Antoine in his room. The shutters are closed. In the darkness he sits on his bed, looking aggravated and gloomy. He hears footsteps coming closer. Soon there is a knock at the door. He doesn't budge. The person outside knocks again and then footsteps are heard going away. Only then does he leap up. He opens the door and jumps back into bed. Colette appears in the doorway.

COLETTE: Listen, boy, I've been knocking at that door for five minutes. You must be getting deaf. It's real dark in here. Are you sick?

ANTOINE: Listen, Colette, we've got to get things straight between us. I can't take these little games of yours . . . I'm sick of the hot and cold treatment.

COLETTE: You're an idiot!

ANTOINE: Sure, I know it's my fault. I should never have moved here, right next to you. As a matter of fact, I'm going back to where I lived before . . . but cut out the games . . . Just leave me alone!

COLETTE: Oh, you're a pain in the neck. I just came to tell you that my parents want you to come over for dinner.

ANTOINE: No.
COLETTE: We won't start for another fifteen minutes, so if you change your mind . . .

Colette closes the door. Antoine remains motionless as he listens to her footsteps fading away.

[31]   The stairway. Antoine is in front of Colette's door. He knocks. She opens the door, munching an apple. With an ironic bow she ceremoniously ushers him into the apartment. He enters the dining room.

THE STEPFATHER: Sit down. Have you had your dinner?
ANTOINE: Yes, yes.
THE STEPFATHER: You're sure?
THE MOTHER: Have you really eaten? I can make you an omelet and some salad. It's no trouble.
ANTOINE: No, really, huh . . . I'll just take a tangerine.
THE STEPFATHER: What's new, Antoine?
THE MOTHER: Are you going out tonight?
ANTOINE: I've got two seats for the Schwarzhof concert, but I'm not sure . . .
THE MOTHER: Well, you two can go there together.
COLETTE: No, no. I can't go.
THE MOTHER: Why not?
COLETTE: Look, it's none of your business.
THE STEPFATHER: The Schwarzhof concert is being televised. I saw it in the program listings.
THE MOTHER: Would you like a plate for the peel?
ANTOINE: No, don't bother. I'll use your plate.

The doorbell rings.

THE MOTHER: What now?
COLETTE: It's a regular parade.

She gets up to open the door as the others follow her with their eyes. Colette comes back accompanied by a young man who is slightly older than Antoine.

COLETTE: Mamma, this is Albert. I've told you about him. This is Antoine. I believe you two have already met . . .
ALBERT: We've seen each other around. Hi!
COLETTE: I'll just be a minute, Albert. I'll get my coat.
THE MOTHER (*to her husband*): Let me have a cigarette, please.
COLETTE: Okay, I'm ready. So long, everybody, we're off.

Colette walks out with her friend, leaving Antoine at the dinner table with her parents. The mother and father seem embarrassed.

THE STEPFATHER: What do you say? Shall we turn on the program?

The three of them settle down in front of the television. On the screen a close-up of Bernard Gavoty as he begins to introduce the musical program.

STOLEN KISSES

(Baisers Volés)

STOLEN KISSES

(Baisers Volés)

CAST AND CREDITS

ANTOINE DOINEL	Jean-Pierre Léaud
CHRISTINE DARBON	Claude Jade
MONSIEUR DARBON	Daniel Ceccaldi
MADAME DARBON	Claire Duhamel
FABIENNE TABARD	Delphine Seyrig
MONSIEUR TABARD	Michel Lonsdale
MONSIEUR BLADY	André Falcon
MONSIEUR HENRI	Harry Max
MADAME CATHERINE	Catherine Lutz
COLETTE TAZZI	Marie-France Pisier
ALBERT TAZZI	Jean-François Adam
THE TELEVISION HOPEFUL	Jacques Robiolles
THE STRANGE MAN	Serge Rousseau

Screenplay, adaptation and dialogue by
François Truffaut, Claude de Givray, Bernard Revon
Directed by François Truffaut
Photography by Denys Clerval
Music by Antoine Duhamel
Production
        Les Films du Carrosse and United Artists

WORK NOTES

Notes from François Truffaut to Claude de Givray and Bernard Revon following their first working sessions and prior to the drafting of the first treatment.

This is the outline of the film as I see it now. But there are several weak spots that still have to be worked out.

[1] We will open the picture in the cell of a military prison, both for the sake of drama and because it affords us the possibility of presenting different types. There are deserters from the professional Army, veterans of the French divisions in Korea and Algeria, there are former criminals and there are also youngsters who failed to report to their draft boards, etc. . . .

Among the "special cases" is Antoine Doinel, who has been declared unfit for service and is being discharged from the Army. We might use this cell scene to illustrate various ways of working up a fever and getting into the infirmary: one guy claims the way to do it is to knock your elbows against the wall for an hour; another says the best way is to smoke cotton mixed with chopped straw, etc. . . .

[2] Antoine is let out of the cell; his discharge has come through. While waiting for the adjutant in the hall, he overhears a briefing on mine detection. Through the half-open glass door (as in *Fahrenheit 451*), he hears the adjutant, in a demagogic monologue spiked with crude innuendoes, compare live mines to women; both

97

have to be handled with great care. Afterward the adjutant takes Antoine to his office and gives him a tongue-lashing, warning him that with a dishonorable discharge from the Army he will have a hell of a time making the grade in civilian life.

It should be made clear that Doinel was not drafted like the others, but that he enlisted of his own volition for a three-year term, probably on account of a girl . . .

His civilian clothes having been stolen, Antoine is forced to hold on to his military uniform, after signing a pledge to return it.

[3] Back to civilian life. First, he must find some civilian clothes; next, he has to get his room back from the friend who's been living there in his absence and is very aggravated at having to move out. The friend lends Antoine some clothes; they're a little too big for him but will do until something better comes along.

[4] Antoine decides to call on Christine, the girl he was in love with before he went into the Army. She is not home, which allows us to set up a scene between the boy and her parents and to maintain some suspense in respect to the girl. So, there is a scene with the parents, from which we gather that before Antoine left for the Army, the parents bought all his books from him (a) to do him a favor, (b) because it was a pretty good deal, and (c) because their daughter wanted them to.

[5] Antoine goes back to his friend, who gives him a lead on a job as a night clerk in a hotel, which would at the same time resolve the problem of the room. The friend can keep the room at night, while Antoine can use it in the daytime. It's the old story about the night watchman and the daily cleaning woman.

[6] The whole sequence in the hotel, up to the adultery scene and Antoine's subsequent dismissal, works pretty well. Still, I have an idea that would improve it; we can discuss it together.

[7]   It is all right for the sequence in the hotel to lead directly to Antoine being hired by the Blady Detective Agency. However, I would like it to happen in a more indirect and unexpected way than what we now have. The old detective should not propose the job to Antoine directly; we should avoid the dialogue and put the audience to work so that it guesses the idea.

[8]   Antoine and Christine get together. Since the character will depend upon the actress who is selected for the role, we shall get back to her at a later date.

[9]   The episode of the affair with the married woman (we can imagine Delphine Seyrig in the role) will begin. Although it involves some complications, I think it would be best to start this episode off with the husband asking the detective agency to conduct an investigation on his behalf (but nothing to do with conjugal jealousy). Antoine is assigned to the investigation, meets the married woman and eventually there is an affair between the two. This might occasion a scene that suggests, perhaps, a bedroom farce— a scene in which the husband, the wife and Antoine are having lunch together. At this point the husband is unaware of Antoine's real function (or perhaps he knows but thinks his wife doesn't know).

[10]   Let us go back to what takes place right after Antoine has said "Oui, monsieur" to the woman who is not yet his mistress. That "Oui, monsieur" is such a dramatic highlight that it cannot be followed by something flat.

The two of them are drinking coffee. For some reason or other the husband is not in the room. Antoine is all keyed up. When the woman says: "Do you like music?" he replies: "Oui, monsieur."

At the moment, all I have in mind for after that "Oui, monsieur" is his flight, underscored by a violent musical passage. Still, the idea of shadowing the woman until she goes into a haberdashery shop sounds good; the scene might wind up with her purchase of the necktie that she arranges to have delivered. After she goes home, Antoine calls the agency to report: "She has gone home and I'm going home too." The next morning a messenger delivers a package to Antoine; it is the necktie, which will rekindle the relationship. Or else we might consider an alternate possibility. Following the "Oui, monsieur," Antoine, humiliated and disgusted with himself, drops the case on the pretext that he's been spotted. Someone else is assigned; it could be the older woman detective, who, tailing the married woman, will find herself in front of Antoine's house. This is one possibility; there are surely others.

From this point onward Antoine is out in the cold. He has quarreled with Christine; his adventure with the married woman has turned sour, and he has lost his job. I must admit that, like Antoine, I'm stumped, for we are faced with several problems:

a. How to wind up the adventure with the married woman.

b. How to make up with Christine (this should be easier).

c. How to work out Antoine's difficulties on the job. I would prefer him not to resign, but to be fired from the agency, and to make sure his dismissal is not handled in a brutal manner.

> Before developing that part of the scenario dealing with the Blady Agency, Claude de Givray and Bernard Revon assembled relevant documentation based on interviews. The following notes to my co-scriptwriters were dictated after my reading of an extensive interview with the head of a private detective agency.

[1]   In the scenes of the Blady Agency I believe that we should use a woman detective, along the lines of the female operative who is mentioned several times in the reports of your interviews with Dubly. To my way of thinking, she should not be too young; she should be older than the married woman in the script. The role

could be played by Catherine Lutz (who played the café owner in
Shoot the Piano Player).

[2]   Some mention should be made in the dialogue of the fact that
whenever two persons are assigned to a case, a man-woman team
is assigned rather than two men, who are easier to spot.

[3]   We can provide some explanations of shadowing techniques
within the agency office by having old M. Henri lead Antoine toward one of the windows and use the passing crowd in the street
below to make his points.

[4]   I believe you dropped the idea of a surname for each dossier.
We should figure out a surname for the dossier of the married
woman. (By the way, I prefer her to be called Fabienne rather than
Cyprienne.) If we retain the notion of the shoe store, "The Cinder-
ella Case" would be an ideal code designation for this case.

[5]   The reason I don't want Antoine to resign from the agency
is that it would be hard to believe and, in any case, not satisfactory,
since we would have to figure out what he will do instead.

The reference to a secretary, to whom Antoine dictates his
report over the phone late in the evening, might be an opening for
the following gimmick. At the height of his affair with the married
woman, Antoine phones in his report and winds up by tendering
his resignation. The following morning M. Henri, who supervises
Antoine's work, figures out a solution; it could be that the husband,
reassured by the initial reports on the previous evening, considers
the investigation is over. I am not certain of this, but we might try
to see whether this idea would work.

[6]   One idea that appeals to me is that at first the report would
be made up of scribbled notations on newspapers, or on a package
of cigarettes . . . This can be used on an evening when Antoine

calls in his report from a public telephone booth, or from a nightclub.

[7]   I think that the true story of the homosexual who goes berserk with grief upon learning that his former boy friend is now a married man and a father is absolutely terrific. We might work it into the picture in this way:

The first time, you would just see the homosexual coming out of the director's office. Antoine would pass him on his way in.

The big scene takes place the second time. We would see him inside the office as he hears the whole story, refuses to believe it and goes berserk. We will show the dentist, from the floor above, trying to calm him down. Possibly, someone might ask the woman detective to take him home. It goes without saying that we will not use a real homosexual to play this role, but a very good actor. The scene must be so genuinely moving that the audience will not snicker.

[8]   Another idea to bear in mind is that of the client who wants the agency to find out why nobody loves him. If we imagine that the client is the husband of the married woman, the motive for his visit allows for a twist that would avoid the stereotype situation, i.e., is my wife unfaithful to me or not?

This man, to my mind, should be very similar to René Morane in The Bride Wore Black and the role might again be played by Michel Lonsdale. The character might suggest someone like Jean Dutourd,* pompous, smug and apparently unaware that his self-satisfaction is the very reason for which he is loathed; this "un-awareness," which seems to be belied by his visit to the Blady Agency, might seem surprising at this point but the concept can be imposed by the right dialogue.

[9]   You will notice that I've dropped the shadowing of the nurse

---

* Jean Dutourd is a Gaullist novelist and newspaperman.

sequence. One thing that bothered me is that it doesn't really fit into the story; in addition, we never find out what the whole thing is really about. But we could keep it in by winding up on a twist I find elsewhere in the interview—the story of the irresponsible nursemaid who casually leaves the children in the sordid *loge**of a drunken concierge after giving her a small tip. It should be clear to the public that the nurse's treatment of the children is shocking. It is not inconceivable, for instance, that she neglects the children to pick up some extra money, during the time she's supposed to be taking them for a walk, by displaying her charms in a twenty-four-hour striptease joint.

[10]   We must hold on to that "Ya Bon Banania"† item and put it somewhere in the film. It's a great way of finding out a person's address and it will work beautifully. We should allow Antoine to pull the trick, but *outside* of his job; he might do it to be helpful to Christine's parents and to show off his professional competence. In a general way Antoine will never be ashamed of his work; he will be a mediocre private eye, but a willing one—unlike Belmondo, who was a reluctant thief in *Le Voleur.*‡

[11]   Without falling into the comic-strip detective genre, we might use the concept of a very simple disguise. Antoine could carry a cap in his pocket and perhaps a pair of eyeglasses, which he can put on, or remove, when he's trying to alter his appearance. In the same vein, we might show the woman operative in the detective agency putting a wig on before going out on a tailing job.

[12]   There might be a funny scene when Antoine is phoning in

---

* In France the living quarters of a concierge are referred to as a *loge*.
† The slogan of a cereal ad that has been a household word in France for some three decades, "Ya Bon Banania" is roughly comparable to "Chiquita Banana" in the United States.
‡ *Le Voleur* (*The Thief*) is a film made by Louis Malle in 1968.

his first report (preferably a verbal one) on the married woman if his physical description of her is such a rave that the secretary, taking it down on the other end of the wire, breaks in with a curt reminder: "We want a report, not a declaration of love . . ."

[13]   The free-for-all in the hotel at the beginning of the film must be described blow by blow, so that the scandal is clearly a put-up job staged by M. Henri.

The cuckold husband should be played by a small, excitable man, whose wild rage is in contrast with the self-assurance of M. Henri. After the husband has broken a mirror with a chair, M. Henri, noticing that he is empty-handed, coolly hands him a vase to break: "Here, monsieur, take this vase . . ."

[14]   In respect to the scene at the Inno store,* I recall Claude de Givray telling us about how people would steal small caviar jars and eat the contents on the premises, in the rest rooms. It might be interesting to have Antoine tell Christine this story when they meet inside the Inno store.

[15]   It is important to make the point that in shadowing a subject, one watches his feet; this is complementary to another professional canon that stipulates that the shadower must carefully avoid meeting the eye of the person he is following.

[16]   It is important to make it clear at the very outset that a private detective is forbidden to pass himself off as a police officer.

[17]   In addition to the detail of the cap the detective carries in his pocket, we might add a jacket that the operative can either wear or carry over his arm whenever he wishes to alter his appearance.

[18]   Claude de Givray reminded us of the following quotation:

* Inno is a Parisian chain of deluxe five-and-dime stores.

A man of genius "is ten per cent inspiration and ninety per cent perspiration." It can be inserted somewhere in M. Blady's dialogue at the time he is explaining to Antoine how a professional detective works.

FIRST TREATMENT*

The picture opens on the face of a military barracks located in the area of the Eiffel Tower. The camera closes in on a heavily barred window of the prison, then moves into the cell where we discover some twelve to fifteen inmates herded together.

The iron door is opened to make way for one of the youngest inmates, Antoine Doinel (Jean-Pierre Léaud). As a result of innumerable violations of Army discipline, he is being discharged as an "unstable element." Antoine is escorted to the office of an adjutant for the routine formalities attending his official release. After informing him that he is getting a dishonorable discharge, the adjutant predicts he will have a tough time making the grade in civilian life because the average employer will not hire a man unless he has an honorable discharge.

Since Antoine's civilian clothes have been stolen, he will have to remain in uniform, after pledging to return it to the Army within thirty days' time.

* This first treatment of Stolen Kisses is so far removed from the final version that it can only be seen as an indication of the step-by-step process. It includes scenes and even characters that were subsequently dropped (before and during the shooting). This being so, it cannot be regarded as a résumé of the final story.

He hops off a bus at the Place Clichy and goes over to one of the buildings where he has a tiny room on the top floor. There he finds his friend Didier, who has been occupying the room during the few months that Antoine was serving his country. What does Didier do in life? He gets by; at the moment he happens to be a house painter. On occasion he bleaches the facades of buildings, thereby doing his bit toward the whitewashing of Paris.

Antoine is flat broke and must find himself a job. Didier gets him one as a night clerk in a small hotel. Antoine cannot afford to turn it down, which is just as well, since Didier will be able to go on sleeping in the room at night, while Antoine can use it in the daytime.

Wearing one of Didier's suits, which is several sizes too large for him, Antoine hurries over to a small house surrounded by a wild garden on the outskirts of Paris.

There, M. and Mme. Darbon, a couple in their forties, give him a warm welcome, but Antoine is clearly disappointed to hear that their daughter, Christine, is out of town on a winter vacation.

As the picture progresses we will see that the relationship between Antoine and Christine, who studies violin at the Conservatoire National de Musique, is so uneven and complex that her parents and his friends are never quite sure where these two stand with respect to each other.

Prior to his enlistment in the Army, Antoine had been deeply infatuated with Christine, who held him at arm's length but never completely shut him out of her life. Following an extensive correspondence with Christine during his military service, Antoine has analyzed the relationship and has finally come to believe that he no longer cares for her.

In any case, Christine's parents are aware that Antoine is alone in life and they manifest their affectionate concern by urging him to stay for supper. Antoine accepts the invitation; during supper he answers their questions about his life in the Army, at the same time managing to satisfy his own curiosity as to what Christine is up to.

For the past week Antoine has been working as a night clerk in the hotel, which allows him ample time for reading. There are no special problems until one morning when two men burst into the lobby at 7 A.M., rousing him from his sleep. They loudly berate the boy for having failed to wake Mme. Colin in room Number 7, with whom they are supposed to leave for London.

Flustered by their vehemence, Antoine takes them up in the elevator and agrees to open Mme. Colin's door for the two visitors. The older of the two men pushes the other one in ahead of him; as soon as he is inside the room the man begins to break everything he can lay his hands on. And with good reason: Mme. Colin, who happens to be his wife, is in bed with her lover! Meanwhile, the older man drags Antoine over to the phone in a corner of the room and persuades him to put in an emergency call to the police.

Alerted by all the racket, the hotel owner walks into the room and sizes up the situation in a glance, guessing that M. Colin's companion is a private detective. Convinced that Antoine has accepted a bribe from the two men, he fires his night clerk on the spot.

In a café around the corner the elderly private detective, M. Henri, explains to Antoine why he had to resort to a frame-up: the courts require that a case of adultery must be verified by a police superintendent, but it takes an endless series of formalities to get one to be on hand at the critical moment. The best way, therefore, is to create a scandal so that the offenders are caught in the act. That mission has now been successfully accomplished.

One thing leads to another and that evening Antoine informs his friends that he has been taken on as a trainee by the famous Blady Detective Agency, which is familiar to most Parisians because of a subway poster showing the black silhouette of a man with his face half-concealed behind a newspaper.

The scenes that follow will illustrate Antoine's debut as a private eye under the guidance of M. Henri. He learns, for instance, that in shadowing a subject, one must avoid his face to watch his feet: the shadower who meets the eyes of the person he is tailing is automatically spotted and must drop from the case.

After theory comes practice: Antoine is assigned to several shadowing jobs on his own.

The first time, he is assigned to follow a woman who, noticing his insistence, thinks he is trying to pick her up and points him out to a policeman. Antoine, without even trying to clear up the misunderstanding, scurries off in the opposite direction.

On another job, the subject he is tailing goes into a post office. While waiting for the man to emerge, Antoine steps into a nearby café to call Christine. Afterward, he goes back to his observation post and it is only when the post office is closing up for the night that he realizes he has goofed once again.

The agency bosses are becoming a little skeptical about their new recruit's professional aptitude but are willing to give him the benefit of the doubt; though he's not much use as a "shadower," it is possible that he might do better as an investigator.

Antoine has seen Christine several times since his return to civilian life. The first time, there is the emotion of getting together again, and there is no problem. The second time, Antoine makes Christine angry when he abruptly remembers that he was supposed to tail someone and runs out of the restaurant right in the middle of dinner. Their third evening together comes to grief when Antoine begins to plead with Christine and covers himself with ridicule besides: just as he is trying to force a kiss upon her in a cinema, the intermission lights come up. Without a word she gets up and leaves him there. Since that disastrous evening, communication between the two has been suspended.

One morning a M. Tabard, the owner of a woman's shoe store, calls on the director of the Blady Agency.

Tabard, a robust-looking man, with the face of a fat cat, acts rather peculiar. It is as if he is not quite sure what he wants the agency to do for him. He talks in generalities and vaguely hints at a plot to victimize him. M. Blady presses him for specific facts. There aren't any but Blady's sympathetic manner encourages Tabard to air his grievances. He used to be vice-president of the Shoe Store Owner's Syndicate but has just lost out in the latest election; his friends make fun of him; his wife doesn't take him seriously; his employees don't respect him, in fact some of them are openly hostile: in a word, he is unpopular, nobody loves him and he wants to know why.

M. Blady assigns Antoine to go to work in the stock room of M. Tabard's shoe shop. There, by mingling anonymously with the other employees, he can see and hear . . . in the professional jargon, he will serve as a "periscope." Two other operatives are assigned to the case: one will sound out M. Tabard's professional circles; the other, Mme. Catherine, a veteran member of the staff, will shadow Mme. Tabard when she is away from the store.

With the complicity of M. Tabard, Antoine is hired as a stock-room boy working in the store basement; he helps the sales-ladies locate the models and sizes of shoes the customers ask for; he also runs errands, some of which give him an opportunity to report the latest information to the agency.

In the store Antoine meets Mme. Tabard, a beautiful, highbred and elegant woman of about thirty-two. He is literally spellbound and wonders how such a superior woman could have married such an inferior man.

That evening, while phoning in his report, Antoine describes Fabienne Tabard in such lyrical terms that the agency secretary understands that Antoine is bewitched by the woman he has been assigned to watch. She curtly suggests that Antoine try to be less lyrical, more precise and simply objective.

Oblivious to his mission in the store, Antoine gazes at his boss's wife in rapt admiration, while Fabienne Tabard, aloof and indifferent, goes about her business: she hasn't even noticed the boy. Eventually, overhearing a conversation between two gossiping salesgirls one day, the young woman is amazed to learn of the new stock-room boy's infatuation for her.

From this moment on, Antoine will find himself in the most agreeable situation there is: an undeclared lover who doesn't know that his beloved is not only aware of his sentiments but is rather touched by them. Yes, Fabienne Tabard finds Antoine's pallor decidedly appealing!

One day, at lunchtime, Antoine is asked to go up to the Tabard flat, above the shop, to get a signature from M. Tabard.

Monsieur and Madame are having lunch; they invite Antoine to join them. He is intimidated and silent. Fabienne Tabard is amiable but reserved. M. Tabard carries on a monologue, trying to convince Antoine that the best way to learn English is to have an English girl friend and tactlessly referring to his many conquests during his bachelor days. After dessert he goes downstairs, leaving his wife and the young man together in a tête-à-tête over coffee.

Antoine is so fascinated by the woman that he is absolutely unable to utter a word. To cover up the long silence Fabienne Tabard puts a record on the turntable phonograph. Looking over toward the boy, she ventures an innocuous question just to make conversation: "Do you like music?"

All keyed up and startled by the break in the silence, Antoine blurts out: "Yes, sir!" In the face of her surprised reaction, Antoine realizes he has blundered. Turning beet red, he simply flees in confusion, without stopping to apologize.

Later that afternoon Fabienne Tabard comes down to the store looking for Antoine. One of the salesladies informs her that he has gone out on deliveries.

Fabienne Tabard puts on her coat, takes her purse and leaves, with Catherine, from the Blady Agency, trailing her footsteps.

That evening Antoine checks in at the agency to make out his report. Mme. Catherine discusses the case with him; she has reason to believe she is on the right track. Having trailed Mme. Tabard the whole afternoon, she saw her go into a haberdashery to buy three neckties. After consulting her address book, she asked to have them delivered, which clearly indicates they were not meant as a present to her husband, but to some other man. Feeling he has been betrayed, Antoine turns white.

When he gets home his concierge hands him a package. Inside his room he tears it open and—lo and behold!—there are three neckties, together with a lovely little note from Fabienne Tabard.

After a few thoughtful moments Antoine sits down to write the young woman a delirious letter, combining thanks, gratitude and amorous rapture. He vows, however, that he will not approach her again: she represents an impossible love; he is unworthy of her . . . In a word, it is the old romantic complaint of the earthworm in love with the star. Rather pleased with his literary prowess, Antoine seals the letter and puts it in the mail.

Early next morning there is a knock at the door. When he opens it, he thinks he is dreaming, for there stands Fabienne Tabard. Fortunately, there is no need for him to say anything for Fabienne is about to explain everything. She talks most convincingly. The reason she is here is that Antoine's letter was at once touching and absurd; she does not want him to approach life with such a theoretical and false concept of love. Women, she explains, are not immaterial beings, nor are they inaccessible: they are made of flesh and blood. Because she feels less inhibited in the semi-obscurity, Fabienne has allowed the room to remain in darkness. Throughout the whole scene we can barely make out Antoine's and Fabienne's faces; their voices convey the action.

The logical conclusion of Fabienne's speech is the gift she is offering to Antoine (and, incidentally, to herself). This will not be the beginning of an affair, but rather a one-time sexual exchange that is at once the outcome of their correspondence and the end of their misunderstanding. The two wonderful hours they spend together will have no follow-up, but they will be very important to the lives of both.

Since Catherine has shadowed Fabienne Tabard to Antoine's house, he is forced to report her visit. M. Blady listens, shaking his head. Undoubtedly the young man has behaved unprofessionally; he has become an active participant in a drama to which he should have been no more than a spectator. The chances are that he's about to be thrown out of the agency.

Inside his office M. Blady continues his tirade with some bitter comments on Antoine's behavior—he wonders out loud whether he will have to hire detectives to watch his own detectives! All of a sudden the door is violently opened by a hysterical secretary: something serious has happened. M. Blady rushes out, followed by Antoine. M. Henri, the elderly detective who supervised Antoine, has collapsed; his head on the desk, he is in a coma. From the phone he still clutches in his hand, a voice can be heard: "Hello, Monsieur Henri. Hello . . ."

The secretary slowly lifts the receiver and says: "Hello, sir. You can hang up. Monsieur Henri is dead!"

Some gravediggers are throwing earth over the detective's grave. M. Blady, surrounded by the members of the staff, is leaving the cemetery. He walks over to Antoine to suggest that he take a few days off. He asks him to report to work the following Monday, adding that he relies on him.

Antoine, at loose ends, wanders through the streets. He notices a prostitute and they go to a nearby hotel. No, she doesn't have to take all her clothes off, he tells her as he stretches out on the bed . . .

That evening Antoine pours his heart out to Didier. He claims he is a lousy son of a bitch; he loved the old man, yet he went to bed with a prostitute one hour after his funeral. Didier reassures Antoine; he himself did the same thing when his grandmother died. It's a normal, logical reaction; to want to make love after death is a way of compensating; it corresponds to the deep-rooted need to create life.

A few days later a curious scene takes place at the Blady Agency. A young homosexual (but not an effeminate one), who had asked for an investigation of a friend who had left him, refuses to believe the agency's report on the case: the friend has just discreetly married a young woman who was about to have a child by him, which explains why he was leading a double life. The young client, unable to accept such an unexpected betrayal, accuses M. Blady of being a blackmailer, of having betrayed his confidence. Then he goes berserk, turns violent, tries to break up everything in sight and fights off all attempts to calm him down. Finally Catherine calls the dentist in the office next door for help and the incident winds up with the dentist bringing the hysterical young man under control.

A few days afterward, in the late afternoon, Antoine takes up a vigil in front of Christine's house. The two have been on the outs since their last disastrous evening together and he doesn't have the nerve to call her, but prefers to run into her accidentally. Taking advantage of his professional training, he sets up an accidental meeting. When Christine leaves her house, he follows her over to an Inno store; there the two of them run into each other.

He helps her with her shopping, discreetly pointing out to her that this or that customer is really a detective; they kid around and pick up where they had left off. Christine asks him to take her home, claiming that she is uneasy because for the past few days a strange man has stationed himself across the street from her house to watch her.

Thus it is that Antoine spends an evening with Christine at her house. The two of them are alone because her parents are away for the weekend. On the pretext of repairing her television set,

Antoine lingers and finally spends the night with the girl, in the parents' double bed.

The following morning Antoine and Christine are exchanging kisses and discussing their plans for a common future on a bench in a small square. A strange man walks up to them. We have seen him several times throughout the picture, following Christine.

Ignoring Antoine, the man declares his love to Christine. He insists that he is the only one who can make her happy, the only one who will be faithful, the only one who would love her as she deserves to be loved. After giving her his name and address and asking her to think it over, he disappears, mysterious as ever.

Watching him walk away, Christine says: "That guy is crazy!" She ostentatiously tears up his card and laughingly throws the pieces away. As he gets up from the bench, Antoine says: "Yes, he must be crazy," but we sense that he is disturbed.

Now, Christine and Antoine go off together. For better, or for worse, they will give it a try.

FINAL SCREENPLAY

PARIS. EXTERIOR. A SUNNY DAY.

The cast and credits unfold over a long shot of the Palais de Chaillot, inside the Trocadero Gardens. The voice of Charles Trenet singing makes up the musical background.

> *The wind in one's hair*
> *Stolen kisses*
> *And shifting dreams*
> *Can anyone say*
> *Where they have gone?*
> *A little village*
> *An old belfry*
> *A lovely view*
> *Hidden away*
> *And in a cloud*
> *The beloved image*
> *Of my past*

A slow panning shot toward the stairway leading to the locked iron gates that open into the Cinémathèque Française. Superimposed over the image is the following text:

116

*This film is dedicated
to Henri Langlois'
Cinémathèque Française
                    François Truffaut*

On the glass doors, behind the gates, there is a sign: "CLOSED. The opening date will be announced in the press."

End of credits.

MILITARY BARRACKS IN PARIS. EXTERIOR. DAY.
A master shot of the Paris area dominated by the Eiffel Tower. We pan over the barrack roofs to frame a porthole window behind iron bars.

A MAN's VOICE (off): Hey! What time is it now?

BARRACKS PRISON CELL. INTERIOR. DAY.
Inside the cell are eight soldiers, including two or three who are older than the draftees and who could be deserters from the Foreign Legion. All the men are in uniform, with the exception of three, who are wearing fatigues. One buck private paces up and down, looking worried. The dialogue is partly offscreen.

A PRIVATE: Ten minutes to four!
ANOTHER PRIVATE: I think you're wasting your time.
ANOTHER PRIVATE (off): What time is it now?

Their conversations overlap as they tell one another how much time they've still got to serve, of different ways to work up a fever and go on sick call, or of what it takes to be declared unfit for service.

A PRIVATE: No, I'm not. In an hour and a half my temperature will be up to a hundred and two.
A VOICE (off): It's nine minutes to four.
ANOTHER VOICE: Try a roll of cotton wrapped in burlap . . .
ANOTHER VOICE: Up your ass!* [Laughter all around.]
THE GUARD: Eight minutes to four!

The camera pans to the side where Antoine Doinel, indifferent to the roughhousing around him, is deeply absorbed in Honoré de Balzac's *The Lily of the Valley*.

A GUARD (off): I've come for Doinel.
A PRIVATE (off): No, there's only one gimmick that really works.
GUARD: Which one is Doinel?
A PRIVATE (off): You mix crushed aspirins with some straw.
GUARD (off): I said: Which one is Doinel?

Antoine looks up and quickly hides his book.

ANTOINE: It's me. Why?
GUARD (off): Over here!

Antoine goes over to the iron-barred door. The guard opens it.

GUARD: Come on.
A PRIVATE: Hey, can I take a leak?
GUARD: No, not until six o'clock.
A PRIVATE: You lousy fink bastard!
GUARD: That'll teach you to beat up the sentry!
A PRIVATE: Hey, Doinel, take a leak for us!
ANTOINE: Okay!
ANOTHER PRIVATE: Hey, get laid for us!

---

* In the French text, "*Quel encule maintenant?*" A rough play on "*Quelle heure est-il maintenant?*"—the words previously used to ask the time.

ANTOINE: Will do!
PRIVATE (off): At five o'clock.

Outside the cell the guard turns Antoine over to another soldier.

ANTOINE (shouts back to the prisoners): At five . . . on the dot!
PRIVATE: We'll be thinking of you at five!

THE BARRACKS. HALLWAY AND STAIRCASE.
INTERIOR. DAY.
Antoine and his escort walk up the stairs and hear the adjutant's voice.

ADJUTANT (off): The anti-personnel mine is smaller than the anti-tank mine. When it explodes, it can inflict serious damage upon any man who happens to be exposed . . .

The escort and Antoine have reached a landing similar to a school corridor. They stop in front of the glass door of a classroom.

ESCORT (to Antoine): Wait here.
ADJUTANT (off): . . . it can destroy the tires of a vehicle . . .

The escort walks into the military classroom.

THE BARRACKS. CLASSROOM. DAY.
Inside the classroom, seated at desks, the privates, with varying degrees of attention, are listening to the adjutant, who walks back and forth in front of them, a mine in his hand. The escort walks over to him.

ADJUTANT: . . . but has no effect on a tank. [Turning to the escort.] What is it?

ESCORT: Private Doinel is here.
ADJUTANT: Just a minute.

The escort stands aside as the adjutant resumes the instruction course, pacing up and down in front of the "pupils."

ADJUTANT: You probe the ground with your bayonet and you say: "What's this? I feel something hard." That's exactly what your girl friend says when you come home on leave, right? Well, dismantling the mine is just like handling a girl—you've got to go easy. You don't walk right up to the girl and put your hand on her ass, do you? No, first you fool around a little . . . Well, it's the same with mines. You've got to go slow. Here, examine it while I'm gone.

Followed by the escort, he goes into the hall, walking ahead of Antoine.

ADJUTANT'S OFFICE. INTERIOR. DAY.

The adjutant sits down at his desk; Antoine faces him, standing up.

ADJUTANT: Well, you finally got it! Good for you! I might add it's just as well for us too . . . it's to everyone's best interests that certain individuals be stopped from cluttering up the Army. Here, look at your service record.

Antoine is not quite sure what expression to assume as the adjutant begins quoting his record out loud.

ADJUTANT (reading off): Private Doinel, enlisted for a three-year term, is hereby discharged from the Army as temperamentally unfit for service. [To Antoine.] I can't figure you out. Some boys simply don't like the Army. They're drafted, they serve their term and that's it. In any case, they never volunteer. Can you tell me why you enlisted?
ANTOINE: Well . . . it was . . . you see, I had personal reasons.
ADJUTANT: Because of some girl. Of course. It's a disgrace! The Army is not a refuge. As if that wasn't bad enough, you've spent your whole enlistment bonus. Actually, I wonder why they don't make you pay it back. If it was up to me . . . I guess you've got connections . . . Communist friends! Those guys run everything nowadays. Well, never mind . . . [The adjutant pauses to study

the booklet, while Antoine conceals a smile.] Assigned to Vidauban . . . went AWOL. For failure to report to Strasbourg, is reported for insubordination . . . Confined to the Dupleix barracks . . . went AWOL. In short, you're always AWOL. You're like Jean de Nivelle's dog, who ran away whenever they called him . . . isn't that right? On top of that, you had your civvies stolen. Your uniform must be returned to us within thirty days. And by the way, your honorable discharge was turned down by order of the general himself. There you are. I suppose you're aware that without an honorable discharge you'll never get into civil service . . . no reliable private firm will hire you. Still, I suppose you can peddle neckties on street corners, but I doubt that you'll sell very many. [*The adjutant hands the booklet to Antoine.*] Well, good luck and here's hoping we never set eyes on you again. Now beat it!

Trying to conceal his laughter, Antoine clicks his heels, turns around and leaves.

PLACE CLICHY. SUNNY DAY. EXTERIOR.

A long shot of the Place Clichy. The camera tracks Number 74 bus until it stops. Antoine, still wearing his military uniform, steps off and looks at his wristwatch. Dodging the cars, he runs across the square. In front of a call house he passes a girl who's walking up and down. He looks her over and walks on. In front of another small hotel two girls and a black man are standing in front of the door. One of the girls coaxes Antoine toward the entrance.

HOTEL. HALLS AND STAIRWAY. INTERIOR. DAY.

On the way in Antoine and the girl pass the glass door of the hotelkeeper. As Antoine begins to go up the stairs, the girl pulls him back. Nervously checking his watch, Antoine walks back toward the two women.

THE GIRL: Where do you think you're going? You've got to pay for the room first.
ANTOINE: Oh, okay!
THE HOTELKEEPER: That'll be eight francs . . . [*Antoine hands her ten. The woman turns to the girl.*] Ginette got picked up again. [*As she's speaking, the woman gives Antoine his change and hands a towel to the girl.*]
THE GIRL: Again!
ANTOINE (*pocketing the change*): Thank you!
THE GIRL: Give her a tip.

Antoine hands the change back to the woman.

ANTOINE: That's for you, madame.

The hotelkeeper continues her gossip with the girl.

THE HOTELKEEPER: It's the third time since Monday. It might be a good idea to bring her some sandwiches over at the police precinct.

Antoine and the girl go upstairs.

THE GIRL: To hell with her . . . she'd better not count on me.
THE HOTELKEEPER (*off*): I can't go . . . I'm stuck here!

ROOM. INTERIOR. DAY.
The door opens; the girl makes Antoine go ahead of her, then locks the door behind him. Antoine grabs her immediately, trying to kiss her on the mouth. She pulls away.

THE GIRL: No, no . . . not on the mouth!
ANTOINE: Why not?

She walks over to the bed, taking off her coat.

THE GIRL: Never with a customer.

Antoine moves over to her; she's wearing a very tight sweater; he tries to caress her hair. She pulls away again.

THE GIRL: Stop messing my hair. I've got spray on.

Antoine caresses her breasts and as he tries to take her sweater off, she pulls away again.

THE GIRL: No, I'm keeping my sweater on. It's cold . . . I'm just getting over the flu. [*She walks over to the sink and turns the water*

on before speaking to Antoine, who is offscreen.] Come here, I'll wash you. [*The sound of a door being opened. The girl looks around in surprise.*] What's the matter. Where are you going?

HOTEL HALLWAY AND STAIRS. INTERIOR. DAY.

In front of the door, Antoine shrugs his shoulders, muttering.

ANTOINE: To hell with her!

On the staircase he runs into another girl who's going down with her customer.

THE GIRL: You can always find me at the Balto. Just ask for Josiane. And if I'm not there . . . just wait ten minutes. Okay?
THE MAN: Right. Why not Saturday?

Antoine, going downstairs, raises his head to look at the girl.

THE GIRL (*off*): Saturday? It's a date, big boy. So long, big boy.
THE MAN (*off*): So long.
THE GIRL (*to Antoine*): Are you coming or going?
ANTOINE: I don't know. Can I go with you?

The girl walks upstairs again, followed by Antoine, who checks his watch and smiles on noticing that it isn't 5 o'clock yet.

THE GIRL: You're my first soldier today. It should bring me luck. What branch are you in?
ANTOINE: Well, I was in the artillery.
THE GIRL: Artillery? Great. I love big guns, honey.

Close-up on an alarm clock in the girl's room indicating that it is 5 o'clock.

PARIS. EXTERIOR. DAY.

Antoine runs across a crowded boulevard as the chimes of a neighboring church clock ring out six o'clock. He hurries over to one of the buildings and steps inside.

ANTOINE'S ROOM. INTERIOR. DAY.

Antoine is home. The room is dark and empty. Next to the door, on a small table, there are two beautiful candlesticks. Antoine takes a toy car from a shelf, blows off the dust and puts it back. He picks up a cigarette butt from an ashtray and after sniffing at it throws it on the floor. He walks around his tiny attic room, goes toward the window and draws the curtains. He comes back to the washbasin and splashes some water over his face and hair. Back to the window, which overlooks the Sacré-Coeur Church in Montmartre. Antoine looks down from the balcony.

A VILLA GARDEN. EXTERIOR. NIGHT.

The gate opens to make way for Antoine, still wearing his uniform. Across the garden and up the steps. He rings the doorbell. The woman who opens the door welcomes him cheerfully.

MADAME DARBON: Oh, Antoine! What a surprise. Come in, come in. Lucien will be surprised to see you.
ANTOINE (off): How is . . .
MME. DARBON (off): Fine.

THE DARBON LIVING ROOM. INTERIOR. NIGHT.

Antoine walks in, followed by the smiling Mme. Darbon. The table is set for dinner.

MME. DARBON: Lucien, look who's here.

DARBON (off): Antoine!
ANTOINE: Good evening, how are you?

Darbon interrupts his meal to get up and warmly shake Antoine's hand.

DARBON: It's been a long time. Good to see you. How are you? Are you on home leave?
ANTOINE: Well, not exactly. I've been discharged. My enlistment's been rescinded.
MME. DARBON: Have you eaten?
ANTOINE: Yes . . . yes . . . don't go to any trouble for me.

They coax him over to the dining-room table.

DARBON: I am sure you haven't had your dinner. Come on, now, join us.
ANTOINE: No, I'm all right. Thanks.
MME. DARBON: Christine will be sorry she missed you. She's not here.
ANTOINE: Oh, that's all right . . .
DARBON: Have you really been discharged? You're not sick, are you? Is it a temporary discharge?
ANTOINE: No, it's a permanent discharge. Instability of character. That applies even in wartime.
MME. DARBON: Well, that's simply wonderful!
DARBON: Oh, the Army, the Army!

Mme. Darbon puts a piece of cheese on a plate, which she puts in front of Antoine.

DARBON: It's just like the theater, a wonderful anachronism.
ANTOINE (lifting his glass): Thank you.
DARBON: Besides, we could never figure out why you enlisted . . . you left so abruptly . . .

MME. DARBON: Lucien, why don't you mind your own business?
ANTOINE: Yes . . . well, I was sort of carried away. I'd read *Military Servitude and Greatness* and I thought it was going to be like that . . .
DARBON: And now you're looking for a job, I suppose.
ANTOINE: Yes, I wouldn't mind finding something.
MME. DARBON: Say, what about Shapiro?
DARBON: What Shapiro?
MME. DARBON: At the Hotel Alsina!
DARBON: Alsina! You're right. I'll call him right away. He's a customer at the garage. He has a hotel in Montmartre. [*While he's speaking, Darbon stands up and moves over to the phone.*] He's looking for a night clerk. The one he had died two days ago. I'll call him now. Would that suit you for a while?
ANTOINE: Oh yes, that would be great.
DARBON: I'll call him.

While he dials the number, the camera frames Antoine and Mme. Darbon at the table.

MME. DARBON: I expect you wanted to see Christine?
ANTOINE: Yes, but it doesn't matter. I can call her tomorrow morning.
MME. DARBON: She won't be home for another week. She's in the mountains, skiing with some friends.

Antoine tries to conceal his disappointment.

MME. DARBON: Did you know the Conservatory's shut down? They replaced the director, but the students preferred the old one and they've been boycotting the courses. It's quite a business!
ANTOINE: I see.

During the conversation, Darbon has been talking on the phone. Now he waves Antoine over.

DARBON: It looks all right. Come and talk to Monsieur Shapiro.

Antoine comes over. Darbon hands him the phone and goes back to the table.

ANTOINE: Hello! Monsieur Shapiro! How do you do?

Darbon whispers to his wife.

DARBON: Say, did I hear you talking about Christine?
MME. DARBON: Yes.
DARBON: What did you tell him?
MME. DARBON: Well, I told him the truth . . . that she's gone off skiing with some friends. What else could I say?
ANTOINE (*into the phone*): Yes, yes . . . fine, good-bye, monsieur.
DARBON (*to his wife*): No, no, it's all right.

Antoine hangs up and walks back toward them.

ANTOINE: Say . . . it's great. Monsieur Shapiro was very friendly. He wants me to go right over.
DARBON: Right now?
ANTOINE: So, if you'll excuse me . . . I think I'd better leave now because . . .
DARBON: You have enough time to finish your cheese.

Antoine takes the piece of cheese from the plate and smiles at them.

ANTOINE: I guess I can manage it.

The three of them move toward the door.

DARBON: Okay, go on, go on. It's worth it. Being a night clerk has its advantages.

ANTOINE: Really?
DARBON: I did it when I was your age. Gives you time to read.

As they cross the threshold, we hear their voices offscreen.

ANTOINE (off): That's great.
DARBON (off): And don't be afraid of Shapiro. He's a nice guy.
ANTOINE (off): Swell.
MME. DARBON (off): I'm going to call Christine and tell her you're here . . . she'll come back.

The screen blacks out.

THE HOTEL LOBBY. INTERIOR. NIGHT.

Behind the reception desk Antoine is comfortably settled in a rocking chair, wrapped in a blanket and reading a pocket book. We can make out the title, La Sirène du Mississipi.* Seen from the inside of the lobby, a girl, Christine, appears in front of the glass door, which is locked, and knocks on it. Antoine lifts his eyes and smiles at Christine, who smiles back at him. Closing the book and taking off the blanket, he stands up and motions for Christine to come in. In sign language she indicates that she can't break the door down. He motions that she should push it in, then puts the book aside, walks around the desk and goes to open it for her. They kiss each other on both cheeks and shake hands.

ANTOINE: Hello, Christine.
CHRISTINE: Hello, Antoine. I'm really happy to see you . . . you haven't changed . . . So you got out of the Army?
ANTOINE: Well, I suppose so . . . yes!
CHRISTINE: That's what my parents said. You must tell me all about it.

* William Irish's Waltz into Darkness.

ANTOINE: Yes, of course. What about you? You just got back today?
CHRISTINE: Yes, this evening. I came right over. Do you like it here?
ANTOINE: It's all right. It's not bad . . . very quiet.

She hands him a round pillbox that contains some vitamins.

CHRISTINE: My parents are afraid you'll catch cold at night, so they told me to bring this.
ANTOINE: What is it? Vitamins. Gee, that's nice, but . . .
CHRISTINE: Yes, yes, take some right away or you'll forget.
ANTOINE: Right. [As he's opening the pillbox, he walks behind the reception desk.] Would you . . . would you like something to drink?
CHRISTINE: Why not. What have you got?
ANTOINE: Let's see . . . there's everything . . . mineral water, Coca-Cola . . .
CHRISTINE: A Coke, yes!

He disappears behind the desk and comes back with two glasses and a Coca-Cola bottle.

CHRISTINE: You know, I was afraid I wouldn't see you anymore. You haven't written me for six months.
ANTOINE: That's right, but most of that time I was in prison or in the hospital . . . besides, at first when I wrote you, you didn't answer most of the time.
CHRISTINE: I did answer, but I couldn't answer all of your letters. There were so many of them! One time I counted them: I got nineteen letters in the same week. I wondered how you could find the time to write.
ANTOINE: Yeah . . . so did I.
CHRISTINE: Besides, they weren't always very nice letters . . . By the way, what's your day off?
ANTOINE: Wednesday.

He takes her to the door.

CHRISTINE: Well then, come to dinner on Wednesday. My parents said to ask you.

They stand outside the glass door.

ANTOINE: Oh, fine. That'll be great, I'd love to. See you Wednesday. Good-bye.
CHRISTINE (*moving off*): Good-bye.

HOTEL ALSINA. EXTERIOR. DAY.
Early in the morning Antoine emerges from the hotel carrying a trash can, which he puts on the sidewalk. Turning around, he sees two men hurrying into the lobby. He rushes in after them.

ANTOINE: Er . . . can I help you?

HOTEL ALSINA LOBBY. INTERIOR. DAY.
One of the men, in his sixties and wearing a hat and a raincoat, seems to be looking for someone. This is M. Henri. The other, in his forties and almost bald, is M. Colin.

HENRI (*waving his cane*): Madame Colin hasn't come down yet?
ANTOINE (*out of breath*): Well . . . I haven't seen anyone yet.
HENRI (*paces nervously back and forth*): I simply don't believe it! Impossible! I have an appointment with her at six, right here, and I'm already late myself. She'll make us miss the train to London and that boat isn't going to stand by for us at Calais . . . She did leave a call, didn't she?
ANTOINE (*dazed*): Listen, I don't know, I'm not sure . . .
HENRI (*handing him the hotel register*): Look, look in your register

. . . Good God! You're not even awake yourself. Let me see . . .
I'll look for myself . . . you're all mixed up . . . Let's see . . .
Six o'clock, Number Eighteen . . . at a quarter to six . . .
ANTOINE (*holding up a card*): Oh, it's Number Twenty-four.
HENRI: Twenty-four? Let's go then. You'd better bring your
passkey . . .

Antoine grabs the passkey and catches up with the two men,
who are already at the elevator.

HENRI: . . . because I know her . . .

Antoine gets into the elevator.

HENRI: . . . she has insomnia . . . she probably took a sleeping
pill. Come on, hurry up. What floor is it?

The elevator goes up with the three men inside.

HENRI (*off*): What floor is she on?
ANTOINE (*off*): The third.
HENRI (*off*): The third . . . If we miss that train, we'll miss the
boat, and if we miss the boat, we'll never get to London.

HOTEL. THIRD-FLOOR LANDING. INTERIOR. DAY.
The elevator stops; the three men get out and head toward
one of the doors. Henri turns toward the third man, who has slowed
down.

HENRI: Come on . . .

Antoine stands in front of the door with his passkey, hesitant
to use it.

ANTOINE: Well . . . this is it . . .
HENRI: Open it.
ANTOINE (*uneasy*): But . . .
HENRI: I told you. She's taken a sleeping pill.

Antoine reluctantly opens the door. They go in.

HENRI: Turn on the light!

HOTEL ROOM. INTERIOR. DAY.
Antoine and Henri walk in first. The light is turned on. The third man is hiding behind Henri. The three men look toward the bed. A young woman emerges from under the sheets and sits up, showing her bare breasts. Antoine turns around to close the door while Henri pushes the confused husband forward.

HENRI: Go on . . . go on, monsieur.

On the bed, Mme. Colin, half-naked, looks unhappy. A sleepy man emerges from the sheets by her side.

MME. COLIN: Julien, what are you doing here?

Henri is still pushing the husband forward.

HENRI: Go on, monsieur . . . go on . . .

Still undecided, M. Colin stares at the guilty couple as if to convince himself of his misfortune.

THE LOVER (*unruffled*): Which one is your husband?

Antoine has turned his back to the scene. His face against the door, he turns slightly and winces at what is going on. The lover sinks down under the sheets again.

THE LOVER: Oh, this is none of my business.
MME. COLIN: What are you doing? Really, Julien . . . this is too much!

The exasperated husband grabs her underclothes from a chair and begins to tear them to pieces.

MME. COLIN: Oh . . . my mother was absolutely right. He is hopeless. Be reasonable, at least. I suppose you think that's clever. I wish you could see yourself in a mirror right now. Just look at him!

Henri goes over to the husband, who's still tearing the lingerie.

HENRI: That's not the way at all, monsieur. That's no good.
MME. COLIN: What good will that do, tell me!

Henri grabs a vase of flowers and hands it to the husband.

HENRI: You can't hear that. It's no good. Here, take this! Go on, break it!

MME. COLIN: Julien, you're out of your mind. Stop it. You're crazy!

Colin pulls the flowers out of the vase and throws them at his naked wife.

MME. COLIN (covered with flowers): I knew it. You're insane!
HENRI (off): No, no . . . not the flowers, monsieur, the vase!

The husband hurls the vase against the wall. Henri, beaming with satisfaction, moves over to Antoine at the door.

HENRI: Ah, that's it. Bravo! Very good, monsieur. Keep it up. That's fine. [*To Antoine.*] Don't just stand there. Call the police. Can't you see he's breaking up the place?

Antoine and Henri hurry out of the room.

HOTEL LOBBY. INTERIOR. DAY.

As the elevator comes down, we hear Henri arguing with Antoine, who is running down the stairs.

HENRI (*off*): I tell you, he's out of his mind. [*Emerging from the elevator.*] Step on it!
ANTOINE: Right away . . .
HENRI: Get on that phone and call the police. And tell them it's an emergency!

Antoine sits down at the switchboard.

HENRI: Tell them it's very serious. That'll make them hurry. Atta' boy. Fine. You're doing great. That's fine.

Antoine dials a number.

ANTOINE: Hello, Fire Department?
HENRI: Not the Fire Department—the police! Number seventeen. Watch what you're doing. [*He takes a bill from his pocket and hands it to Antoine.*] Here, this is for you. Take it. You can get yourself some candy . . . what you like.
ANTOINE: Hello, police?
HENRI: That's it.
ANTOINE (*handing the bill back to Henri*): Uh . . . I'm calling from the Alsina, 39 Avenue Junot. [*The bill is handed back and forth.*] Look . . . something's going on on the third floor.

HENRI: Tell them they're breaking everything up.
ANTOINE: Well, they're breaking everything up in a room on the third floor.
HENRI: Don't be nervous . . .
ANTOINE: Huh. Good. Right away.

Antoine hangs up. Henri, looking very pleased, shoves the money into Antoine's hand and starts to leave. Antoine walks around the desk after him.

HENRI: Keep it . . . it's yours.
ANTOINE: I don't want it.

The director of the hotel, looking very angry, goes up to both of them.

THE DIRECTOR: What's going on around here?
ANTOINE: I don't understand it, monsieur. Some man just surprised his wife . . .
HENRI: Right.
ANTOINE (*stammering*): You know . . . the lady in Twenty-four. Well, she was with Number Nineteen.
THE DIRECTOR: And you opened the door for him?
ANTOINE (*bewildered*): Well, this man told me . . . well, he said to hurry . . .
DIRECTOR (*to Henri*): Oh, I get it . . . a private detective?
HENRI (*moving toward the door*): That's right.

The director begins to shove him out.

HENRI: All right . . . I'm going . . . all right.

The director now turns back to Antoine, who stands there, petrified, the money in his hand. He grabs it from him.

THE DIRECTOR: You'd better go with him. [*He tears the bill in two and hands one half to Antoine.*] That's your separation pay [*he hands him the other half*] and this is your Christmas bonus.

CAFÉ. INTERIOR. DAY.

We are in a café near the Hotel Alsina. Antoine comes in and walks over to the counter, ordering a fruit juice.

HENRI (*off*): Hey you . . . young man . . . young man!

Antoine turns in surprise, then walks over to Henri.

HENRI: Sit down. What'll you have?

Antoine sits down next to Henri. He is carrying his book, *La Sirène du Mississipi*, and the box of vitamin pills.

ANTOINE: No thanks. I ordered something at the bar.
HENRI: Doesn't matter.
ANTOINE: You sure pulled a fast one!
HENRI (*feigning surprise*): Me? What do you mean?
ANTOINE: You're a private detective.
HENRI (*smiling*): Oh, that! I've been working for the Blady Agency for the past thirty years. [*To illustrate what he means, he grabs a newspaper and hides the lower part of his face behind it.*] You know it?

Antoine, looking doubtful, shrugs his shoulders.

HENRI: You must have seen their publicity on the . . .
ANTOINE: No . . . no . . .
HENRI: . . . on the back cover of the directory [*imitating the ad*] . . . the man who looks like this [*again he conceals the lower part of his face*].

ANTOINE: Oh sure, I remember now.

HENRI: Well, that's it. For instance, last night, you didn't know it, but I was in the lobby of your hotel. Nobody noticed me. In fact, I was there when Madame Colin and her boy friend went upstairs to their room. So I knew we would find them in bed together. But I still needed the testimony . . .

ANTOINE: In that case, why didn't you call the cops right away?

HENRI: Well, because they wouldn't have come. First, my client, Monsieur Colin, would have had to make a complaint to the D.A.'s office; then the D.A. would have had to notify the police . . . you see?

ANTOINE: Yes, but what happens when the police get there?

HENRI: Well, you see . . . the cops make an official report that at a certain hour they witnessed a Monsieur Colin entering a hotel room and taking the law into his own hands by assaulting two people who were in bed together, one of these persons being, as it happens, Monsieur Colin's lawful wife. Mind you, theoretically, the cops are supposed to handle disturbances at night. But in this way we've got all the proof we need to establish adultery.

ANTOINE: Not bad . . . not bad . . .

HENRI: So that's the job. Which reminds me, I've got to go. Come on. [*They go over to the door, still talking.*] I was supposed to make a phone call. Well, never mind, I can make it from the office. Meanwhile, you've lost your job. It's a shame.

ANTOINE: Well, you know . . . that's life. Go ahead.

HENRI (*going out*): Thanks. Good-bye all.

On the sidewalk the two shake hands. Henri walks on, then stops, turns around and calls Antoine, who runs over to him. The two talk together. Music.

PARIS. AN AVENUE. EXTERIOR. DAY.

Concealing his face behind *Le Monde*, which is turned upside down, Antoine is shadowing a pretty young woman who's walking ahead. From Antoine's POV we see her walking ahead of him and then discreetly turning around. Antoine darts over to hide behind a doorway. The girl, still walking ahead, is followed by Antoine, who zigzags, occasionally concealing his face behind the paper. The young woman, having noticed that she's being followed, crosses diagonally at a square and goes up to a traffic cop. She points Antoine out to him. Antoine tries to hide behind a lamppost. The cop motions Antoine over. Frightened, Antoine runs off in the opposite direction with the cop blowing his whistle after him.

PARIS STREET. EXTERIOR. DAY.

On the sidewalk, Christine is being followed by a strange man in a raincoat. She is carrying a violin case. Finally she reaches the gate of the Darbon home and walks in without shutting the gate. The man stops and stares inside as she goes up the steps and into the house.

DARBON LIVING ROOM. INTERIOR. DAY.

Christine comes in and puts her violin on a shelf. Lucien Darbon is in an armchair reading *Auto-Journal*.

CHRISTINE: Hello, Lucien.
DARBON: Hello, Christine.
CHRISTINE: Is Mother back yet?
DARBON: No, no, the trains are on strike. She won't get in till tomorrow, but we'll be three for dinner anyway. Look who's behind you!

She turns around and moves toward Antoine, who is standing next to the bookcase with a book in his hand.

CHRISTINE: Why, it's Antoine. How are you?
ANTOINE: How are you, Christine?
CHRISTINE: I expected you on Wednesday. Aren't you at the hotel anymore?
DARBON: He doesn't work there anymore. He's been fired.
CHRISTINE: Oh . . . then he's looking for a job?
ANTOINE: No, no. I've already found one.
CHRISTINE (*to Darbon*): What is he doing?
DARBON: Oh, you'll never guess. Go on, try . . . guess . . .
CHRISTINE: I don't know . . . selling newspapers?

Antoine smilingly shakes his head in the negative.

DARBON: Oh, no . . . he's doing better than that. Try again.

Antoine leafs through the book as Christine looks at him with a puzzled expression on her face.

CHRISTINE: A porter at Orly . . . that's not so bad!
DARBON: You need connections for that. No, that's not it.
CHRISTINE: I have no idea . . .
DARBON: Go on, use your imagination!
CHRISTINE: A . . . painter?
DARBON: It doesn't pay!
CHRISTINE: Writer . . .
DARBON: Oh, no, no, no, this pays more!
CHRISTINE: It pays more?
DARBON: Keep guessing.
CHRISTINE: Water taster?
DARBON: What an idiot! She'll say anything.
CHRISTINE: Why not, it's a wonderful job. I saw it on television.
DARBON: No, that's a very exclusive profession. This is . . . much easier.

Antoine is enjoying his complicity with Darbon.

CHRISTINE: A night cabdriver?
DARBON: Ah . . . we're getting a little closer this time. Come on, guess again.
CHRISTINE: A poet?
DARBON: No . . . worse than that.
CHRISTINE: Worse?
ANTOINE: (laughing): Why not a necktie salesman?
DARBON: Less intellectual . . . more dangerous!
CHRISTINE (shrugging): Well . . . I give up.
DARBON: I said dangerous.
CHRISTINE: Dangerous? I'm stumped.

DARBON: Shall I give you a hint? If I do this . . . [*Darbon mimics a man using a magnifying glass as if to detect something.*]
CHRISTINE: Is it a gun?
DARBON: (*bursting into laughter*): No, it's not a gun; it's a magnifying glass!

Antoine and Christine join in the laughter.

DARBON: A big magnifying glass.
CHRISTINE: A magnifying glass?

Back to Darbon, who repeats his mimicry and nods to Antoine to help Christine.

CHRISTINE: I have no idea . . .
DARBON (*to Antoine*): Go on.
ANTOINE: I'll give you a clue . . . Look! [*Antoine turns his lapel over.*]
CHRISTINE: Oh, a sheriff!
DARBON: You've got it. Didn't you notice his horse in the garden?
CHRISTINE: Stop kidding me.

Antoine grabs the phone directory and points to the Blady Agency ad on the back cover.

ANTOINE: Yes, yes. No, we're not kidding. It's true, I work at a detective agency.
CHRISTINE: A private eye?
DARBON: That's right. Meet Antoine Bond of the FBI.
ANTOINE (*in a more serious vein*): No . . . euh . . . You know it. The Blady Agency. Investigations, searches, shadowing.
CHRISTINE: Oh, so that's it. That's terrific! Congratulations. You can tell us all about it at dinner. Come here and help me.

The camera pans over to the door as the two youngsters leave the room.

CELLAR STAIRCASE. INTERIOR. EVENING.

Christine walks down the steps followed by Antoine.

CHRISTINE: Antoine, I won't be able to spend the whole evening with you. I've got to meet some friends after dinner.
ANTOINE: I see . . .

They move over toward the stacks of wine bottles. She turns to face him.

CHRISTINE: Do you mind?
ANTOINE (*taking two of the bottles off the stacks*): No, no, I don't mind at all.
CHRISTINE: Are you really sure . . . because . . .
ANTOINE: I tell you I really don't mind. I don't mind a bit.
CHRISTINE: And if you did mind, would you tell me?
ANTOINE: No, I wouldn't tell you if I minded . . . but I really mean it . . . I don't mind at all.

He looks at her and then awkwardly raises his hand to caress her face, comes closer and gently kisses her. When he pulls away, she is smiling. He moves forward again, shoving her up against the wall in a passionate embrace. When they pull apart, her hair is slightly disheveled. In silence she begins to walk up the stairs. He takes the two bottles and follows her up.

FOYER OF THE DARBON HOME. INTERIOR. EVENING.
Before stepping into the living room Christine fixes her hair in front of the mirrored door. Antoine precedes her into the room.

LIVING ROOM. INTERIOR. EVENING.
Darbon is setting the table; Antoine hands him the two bottles. Jokingly, he grabs Antoine by the jacket and pretends to rough him up.

DARBON: Come on, come on . . . start singing!
ANTOINE (*goes along with the joke*): I'm no canary!
CHRISTINE: Objection, your Honor!
ANTOINE: Watch it, you two. Anything you say can be used against you!

While Christine finishes setting the table, Antoine walks over to the door and closes it in the face of the camera.

BLADY'S OFFICE. INTERIOR. DAY.
A big office, with velvet drapes and padded doors. The boss is studying some papers at his desk.

BLADY: Good, I'm very pleased with you, Catherine. You did a good job on that investigation in London . . .

As he talks, the camera gradually reveals his staff: M. Julien, around forty, Mme. Catherine, M. Henri (seated) and a secretary who is taking notes of the meeting. Antoine stands to one side.

BLADY: But was it really necessary to have all of your meals on room service?
CATHERINE: Monsieur, I don't know whether you know the Hilton hotel in London, but it's situated at an angle, so that from my window I was able to see him going out and coming back . . .
BLADY: Any developments on that dry-goods case at the St. Pierre market?

During the ensuing discussion, Catherine begins to apply nail polish.

JULIEN: Nothing new. It's impossible for that saleslady to take anything home. I've followed her from the store to her house for three weeks. She can't hide anything under her coat and she carries a tiny purse. I tell you one thing: that woman's not a thief. I simply can't figure it.
BLADY: Okay . . . we'll drop it for the time being, because I think I know what it's all about. [He stands up to pace the floor.] I'm almost sure her boss made the whole thing up. It's not because she's

stealing that he wants to find out what she's up to, it's because he's in love with her. He's looking for some information that would help him to enter her life. He's simply got a crush on the girl and was too embarrassed to tell me the truth.

CATHERINE: It's a little like that guy in the Agricultural Ministry three years ago . . .

Blady walks back toward the group.

BLADY: That's right, but remember what happened to him! [*He mimics a man putting a gun to his head and pulling the trigger.*] Bang! Bang!

HENRI (*laughing*): Bang! Bang! Why bang? That guy hung himself.

BLADY: He did not. He shot himself in the head.

HENRI: I'm sorry, but he hung himself from a beam in the Ministry attic . . .

Henri, followed by the other members of the staff, moves toward the door. Blady goes over to Henri.

BLADY: When you hang yourself . . . the brains are not splattered all over. I know what I'm talking about.

HENRI: . . . with the sash of his bathrobe.

They all leave with the exception of Antoine, who can't get out because Henri stands in front of the door.

BLADY: Of course, Henri, you always have to have the last word.

HENRY: Sure! I was arguing with your father when you were in short pants!

BLADY (*holds Antoine back*): No, no, Doinel. You stay here.

Antoine walks back into the office as Blady goes on talking to Henri.

BLADY: Yes, but my father had lots of patience with you. So do I, but there are limits . . .
HENRI: Of course . . . there are . . . limits . . . to patience.

As he walks out of the office, Catherine steps back to the door.

CATHERINE: Excuse me, Monsieur Albani is here for his appointment.
BLADY: Oh, yes, show him in. [*To Antoine, as he waves him out of the office.*] Listen, I'll see you in a little while. Don't go away.

Antoine goes outside as Catherine comes back with the client. M. Albani walks into the office.

ALBANI: How do you do, monsieur.

HALLWAY OF THE BLADY AGENCY. INTERIOR. DAY.
Antoine paces back and forth in front of Blady's office. Catherine passes him on her way out.

ANTOINE: Good-bye, madame.
CATHERINE: Good-bye, monsieur.

She slams the door behind her. M. Paul, passing through the hall, speaks to Antoine.

PAUL: Waiting for the boss?
ANTOINE: Yes, I am.
PAUL: Don't stand there. Come in and sit down.

Antoine follows Paul into the detectives' office and sits down next to the open door.

BLADY'S OFFICE. INTERIOR. DAY.

Albani, tall, well-groomed, neat, and in his early thirties, looks distressed as he tries to explain his problem to Blady. Pencil in hand, Blady, seated at his desk, is listening to Albani.

ALBANI: Well, you see . . . it's about a friend who was staying with me [*Blady takes notes.*] About a month ago he disappeared without leaving an address. He left his things behind . . . clothes, books and other things . . . I'd like to forward them to him.
BLADY: In other words, you'd like us to find him.
ALBANI: Yes, but you see, it's a little more complicated than that. I'm also interested in finding out what kind of life he's been leading . . . you understand [*Albani's hands betray his nervousness.*] . . . what he's doing . . . who he sees . . .

Blady takes a discreet look at his client's hands and then speaks up very gently.

BLADY: Yes, I understand perfectly. Well, we will find out his address and will have him followed. We'll carry out a thorough investigation. It will cost you . . . euh . . . three hundred francs a day.
ALBANI: Splendid . . . splendid . . . but how long do you think . . . Will it take a long time?
BLADY: Well, that depends on how easy . . . your friend's address . . . whether it's easy to find the gentleman's address or not. What does he do for a living?
ALBANI: He is a night club magician. [*A close-up focuses on Albani's hands.*] He does a number with little colored cords.

DETECTIVES' OFFICE IN THE BLADY AGENCY.
INTERIOR. DAY.

Through the open door we see Antoine and Paul facing each other at a desk and working out a puzzle in the newspaper.

PAUL: Yes, I always do the crossword puzzle as an exercise. Too bad they're so easy.

The secretary passes through and stops to knock at the door of Blady's office.

BLADY'S OFFICE. INTERIOR. DAY.
Blady and Albani are standing.

BLADY: Come in. I want to dictate something to you.

The secretary steps in. Blady escorts Albani to the door and opens it as they talk.

BLADY: Fine. We'll get started right away. Call me in a few days.
ALBANI: All right. Thank you, monsieur. Good day.

Blady closes the door behind Albani, but goes over to the detectives' office before returning to his own.

BLADY: Is Doinel there?
ANTOINE (off): Yes, monsieur. Yes, monsieur.

In the hallway separating the two offices Blady and Antoine pace up and down as they talk.

BLADY: Yes, I wanted to ask you . . . first . . . are you quite sure you understand yourself?
ANTOINE: Oh, yes, yes.
BLADY: Because, you see, I've got to understand you too. You must realize, Doinel, that we are not the official police. We are not under oath here. We must never try to pass ourselves off as members of the police force. True . . . in our work we need initiative and

cunning. In fact, our profession is ten per cent inspiration and ninety per cent perspiration.

AN APARTMENT HOUSE. INTERIOR. DAY.

Henri and Antoine are talking together in front of the concierge's door.

A series of rapid shots showing Antoine's initiation under the guidance of Henri. Stairways, courtyards and streets.

Antoine, carrying an umbrella, is on a stairway landing with a stocky man. He rings the doorbell. Antoine, alone, is ringing another doorbell. Next, Antoine wearily climbing up a staircase and looking down. At the landing, he rings and the door is opened by a pretty young woman. Henri and Antoine together in front of another doorway that is opened by an older woman. Antoine also in front of a door that is opened by a big, surly-looking man. Henri is waiting in the lobby of a big building. Antoine runs over to him and we gather from his gestures that he was unsuccessful in whatever he was trying to do upstairs. On a landing, Henri and Antoine stand in front of a door. This time Henri is carrying the umbrella. There is no response to their knock and he shrugs his shoulders. Antoine, by himself, in front of another door that opens briefly, only to be shut in his face.

From the doorway of an elegant building, Henri and Antoine, seen from the back, are watching the doorway across the street. A distinguished-looking man comes out and they conceal themselves.

As the distinguished-looking client gets into his car, Antoine crosses the street and hails a cab. Henri joins him.

TAXI. INTERIOR. DAY.
Antoine and Henri are in a cab that's driving through Paris. Henri points to a café.

HENRI: See that little joint . . . on Thursdays they serve ham hocks with lentils.

The camera reveals that their cab is following another car.

THE DARBON HOME. EXTERIOR. NIGHT.
Antoine, on the stoop, rings the doorbell. Mme. Darbon opens the door.

MME. DARBON: Oh, good evening, Antoine.
ANTOINE: Good evening. I've come to see Christine.
MME. DARBON: She isn't here.
ANTOINE: Oh, well, I'd better be going then.

She holds him back.

MME. DARBON: No, no. Come in for a few minutes. Have some coffee.

She pulls him inside and shuts the door just as a pan shot moves over to the outside door of the cellar from which Christine emerges. Wearing gloves and dressed up as for a date, Christine bends down to avoid being spotted from the windows as she hurries toward the garden gate.

THE DRESSING ROOM OF THE BLADY AGENCY.
INTERIOR. DAY.

In the room, which leads to the rest rooms, we find Catherine and Paul in each other's arms, exchanging a long kiss.

PAUL: What about tonight? Can I come over?
CATHERINE (*pulling away*): No, I said Saturday and I mean Saturday. [*On the way out she grabs a hairbrush.*] And if you don't like it, we don't have to see each other at all.
PAUL: No, no . . . Saturday's all right with me.

Paul combs his hair in front of the mirror as Antoine comes in to do the same.

ANTOINE: Boy, you sure look funny. What's wrong?
PAUL: It's Catherine. One can't live with that one. I've never heard of a woman who doesn't want to get married.
ANTOINE: Well, it's the same here. I've been chasing this girl for two years now. I know I'm never going to get anywhere with her. Why don't you lay a whore?
PAUL: I can't take them. They're too dirty.
ANTOINE: Oh . . . euh . . .
PAUL: When I was your age I ate French fries in the street. I laid girls who needed a bath, and whose bras were held together with safety pins. Today I can't take that anymore. In a way, it's too bad.
ANTOINE: Well, I've got a terrific date . . . a very tall girl. What do you do when . . . I mean when the girl is taller than you are?
PAUL (*fixing his tie*): I often have that kind. I don't do anything special.
ANTOINE: Is that so? But I mean a really tall girl . . . very tall. In the street it's a bit . . . if she's too . . . you know . . .
PAUL: In that case there's only one way to handle it: you've got to look professional!

STREET. EXTERIOR. DAY.

From the back we see Antoine walking along the sidewalk next to a pretty blonde, a good deal taller than he is. He keeps his hands in his pockets and seems to be talking profundities. The couple reach the corner and disappear around it.

PLACE DE L'OPÉRA. A SUBWAY ENTRANCE. EXTERIOR. NIGHT.

As Paul and Antoine talk together, the former is leaning against the rail of the stairway leading down to the subway, while Antoine, his hands in his pockets, paces back and forth in front of Paul.

PAUL: How did it work out with the girl?
ANTOINE (sighing): At first it was sad, downright depressing. But later on . . . it was terrific! The walls were really shaking. Fantastic . . . it was real wild!
PAUL: Well, you see. You know, when my grandfather died—it was in Nemours—I felt terrible. My cousin too . . . she was crying her eyes out.
ANTOINE: Yeah . . .
PAUL: There was one of those big family meals . . . like they always have in the country. [They begin to go down into the subway.] Well, right after dessert, we went up to the attic together and I laid her right there . . . on the floor.
ANTOINE: Go on!
PAUL: Well, just imagine if someone had caught us. They would have thought we were monstrous. Since then I've often thought about it. Making love after a death is like a way of compensating `. . . as if you need to prove that you still exist.

THE DARBON GARAGE. INTERIOR. LATE AFTERNOON.

Antoine enters the garage and, passing the mechanics at work, heads for the office. Inside, Mme. Darbon is sitting at the desk. She takes off her dark glasses and shakes Antoine's hand.

MME. DARBON: Hello, Antoine.
ANTOINE: Hello, madame.
MME. DARBON: Christine isn't here yet, but she won't be long. Are you two having dinner with us or are you going straight to the movies from here?
ANTOINE: Oh, no . . . tonight I'm taking her to a club in the Latin Quarter. I've got to go there in connection with an investigation.
MME. DARBON: Oh, that's right. You're a detective. It must be fascinating work.

Pacing up and down, Antoine launches on an animated description of his work.

ANTOINE: Yes, why only this afternoon, a very strange thing happened. There was this woman, the mother of twins, who came to the agency because . . . well, though the nursemaid was walking the children in the afternoon, it didn't seem to do them much good. She couldn't figure out why the twins were so skinny and so pale . . . She couldn't watch the nurse herself because she works, but she wanted to find out what was going on. So I was assigned to follow her. Well, this afternoon, I wait for the nurse in front of the lady's apartment house. She finally comes out with the twins. She walks for a while and then goes into a little square. I'm right behind them.

Darbon comes into the office looking very busy.

DARBON: Well, well, you're here, Antoine.
ANTOINE: Oh, hello.
DARBON: How are you? [He feverishly searches through the desk drawers.] What did I do with that thing . . . [To Antoine.] Oh,

that's right, you're here to meet Christine . . . [*He goes out again.*]
MME. DARBON (*impatiently*): Well, well . . . she got to the
square . . .
ANTOINE: So she crosses it without stopping and comes out at the
other end with the twins. Then she goes inside a doorway and leaves
the babies with a concierge in a fifthy, sordid, stinking *loge*. Then
she comes out by herself, crosses the Boulevard de Clichy and
walks into a striptease joint.
MME. DARBON: In a what?

As he explains, Antoine mimics a striptease number.

ANTOINE: Yes, yes . . . in a striptease joint, where she stripped off
her nurse's uniform. I mean she did her number as a nurse . . .
like this . . . two or three things with the baby's bottle . . . You
see, it's a nonstop show . . .
MME. DARBON (*fascinated*): Yes!
ANTOINE: Fifteen minutes later she did her act again. I mean it!
After that she went back to the concierge's place, picked up the
twins, handed the woman a little money . . . a tip, I guess . . .
and took them home.
MME. DARBON: I can't believe it! No wonder they looked so pale!
ANTOINE: Then I made up my report . . . and I've just called it in
to Suzanne.

Christine walks into the office, followed by Darbon.

MME. DARBON: It's incredible!

While Christine greets Antoine, Darbon begins to search
through the drawers of the desk again.

CHRISTINE: Hi, Antoine. Have you been here long?
MME. DARBON: You bet! He's been waiting for the past two hours.

ANTOINE: No, not that long.

MME. DARBON (*to her husband*): What are you looking for?

DARBON: It's a pain in the ass! I can't find the address of the Langmans. [*He goes on searching.*] He did me a favor and I want to send his wife some flowers.

MME. DARBON: Well, just call him up. We've got his phone number.

DARBON: You're a big help. Wouldn't I sound like a damn fool if I call Langman and say: "Hey, old man, give me your address so that I can send you some flowers."

ANTOINE (*assuming a professional manner*): Look, if I understand it correctly, you have his phone number but you want his address. Is that right?

MME. DARBON: Yes . . . Langman . . . 525–55–73.

ANTOINE: Then there's no problem. I can take care of it.

Standing in front of the Darbons, Antoine picks up the phone and dials a number. Darbon looks worried.

DARBON: What are you doing, Antoine?

Christine and her mother hush him.

ANTOINE: Hello . . . 525–55–73? Madame Langman?

In the background Mme. Darbon and Christine look puzzled.

ANTOINE: How do you do, madame. Look, if I say "Chiquita," what do you say? [*A pause.*] Banana? You are right. Congratulations, madame, you have just won five kilos of bananas! [*Speaking loudly, in the manner of the radio commercial announcers.*] To what address should we deliver them, please?

Darbon takes out his notebook.

ANTOINE: Six Rue Ribera? Very good and thank you. Thanks again and congratulations!

Antoine hangs up. After writing down the address, Darbon turns to him.

DARBON: Hey, that was terrific. Very clever!
ANTOINE (*assuming an air of false modesty*): Oh, it's just one of the tricks of the trade!
CHRISTINE: Well, are you taking me to the movies?
ANTOINE: No. Tonight I've got to do a little job in a cabaret in the Latin Quarter. They tell me the show there is great. Do you mind not going to the movie?
CHRISTINE: Not at all. On the contrary . . .

The four of them walk out of the garage.

CHRISTINE (*in a lower voice to Antoine*): If it's a place where the lights are on, you will behave yourself and leave me alone!

CABARET. INTERIOR. NIGHT.
Antoine and Christine are at a table, side by side. Christine is wearing a white dress and Antoine is in a dark suit. On the table there are two glasses of Coca-Cola. Music in the background. As the lights are dimmed, both of them look over toward the stage. The curtains are drawn and a man in his mid-thirties, wearing a tuxedo, stands in the middle of the scene. He is a prestidigitator. He holds a colored silk cord in his hands, deftly makes a series of knots that disappear when he waves the cord. Some of the spectators applaud.

THE PRESTIDIGITATOR (*keeps on making knots while delivering his spiel*): Once upon a time, there was an old mariner on his last voyage, a magician, a storyteller. [*Christine discreetly takes hold of Antoine's hand.*] He was ageless, in fact, he's still alive. He was

known as a fabulous personage. [*He pulls a pink scarf out of the cord.*] The children still listen to his tales, sitting on the steps of the old port. As he played with his cords, he would revive colorful legends. [*The prestidigitator unties his cord, which turns red as the silk scarf disappears.*] He had cords of all kinds. He had cords of all lengths . . .

Panoramic from the stage to the table, where Antoine is timidly caressing Christine's hand.

THE PRESTIDIGITATOR: He had cords of all colors. He had white ones. He had red ones. Some were green and some were yellow. They were tangerine, Bordeaux red, purple and blue . . .

Back to the table. Antoine pulls his hand away, takes a pencil out of his pocket and begins to make notes on the prestidigitator.

THE PRESTIDIGITATOR: We saw him . . . you remember . . . under the full moon in June. He would coil the golden cord and place it by his side. And then, as if it were a ritual . . . as though he'd found something . . . who knows . . . a forgotten science . . . we saw him slowly, carefully, tie a knot in the blue cord. Then he coiled the cord around in his fingers. The knots, he said, would leave the blue cord to tie themselves into the golden one . . . [*During this spiel, the prestidigitator continues his manipulations of the cord.*] Then, he would send them from the gold back to the blue.

Applause greets the end of his act. He bows. Antoine puts some money on the table, gets up abruptly and turns to Christine.

ANTOINE: Excuse me . . . I'm really sorry about this, but I've got to go now. It's for my job.

Christine is rather taken aback as Antoine goes off. On the stage the performer is taking more bows as the audience applauds.

Weaving his way through the tables, Antoine heads for the check-room. Before going out he turns to give a last look at the presti-digitator.

STREETS. EXTERIOR. DAY.

Antoine, concealed behind a tree, is watching the wrought-iron door of an impressive apartment building. He comes to attention as a silhouette appears behind the door, which opens to make way for the prestidigitator. As he passes the tree, Antoine circles around it so as not to be seen. The man walks on, with Antoine following in his footsteps. When the man turns around, as if sensing a presence, Antoine stops and after putting on a cap resumes his shadowing. They reach a post office building. The man goes up a few steps and disappears inside as Antoine, after peering through the windows, crosses the street to take up his vigil next to a telephone booth on the sidewalk. Antoine stamps his feet, rubs his hands together, takes a few steps, with his eyes glued on the post office entrance. Next to him a young couple, with the husband carrying their baby in his arms, prepares to cross the street. Suddenly the young woman turns around in surprise.

COLETTE: Antoine . . . my goodness, this calls for a big kiss.*

She kisses Antoine on both cheeks.

COLETTE (*turning to her husband and smiling*): Albert, you re-member Antoine?

Albert, a little embarrassed, nods vaguely as his wife makes a grand introduction.

* This sequence is a throwback to Love at Twenty, in which again Marie-France Pisier played Colette, Antoine's first love.

COLETTE: Antoine Doinel . . . Albert, my husband!
ALBERT: Oh, yes. Hello.
ANTOINE: Hello.
COLETTE: What are you doing around here?
ANTOINE (*looking over toward the post office*): Oh, just waiting for a friend.
COLETTE: I see.

Antoine caresses the baby's face with his finger.

COLETTE: I bet you're are wondering if it's a boy or a girl. You must come over one of these evenings and have dinner with us, isn't that so, Albert?
ALBERT (*in a noncommittal voice*): Yes, of course.
COLETTE: Did Mamma give you my new phone number?
ANTOINE: Euh . . . yes . . . yes . . . I think so.
COLETTE: Well, you didn't exactly knock yourself out to get in touch with me, did you? In the old days you weren't so bashful about using the telephone, remember? Well, we'll be seeing you. So long.
ANTOINE: Good-bye.
ALBERT: Good-bye, sir.

As the couple goes off, Antoine throws another look at the post office entrance, then abruptly steps into the telephone booth with glass panels. Holding his hat in his hand, and looking over to the post office from time to time, he dials a number.

ANTOINE: Hello, Christine?
CHRISTINE (*off*): Yes.
ANTOINE: Hello, it's me . . . Antoine.
CHRISTINE (*off*): Oh, hello.
ANTOINE (*feverishly*): Look, I'm calling because . . . the last time . . . I had to leave rather suddenly. I hope you're not angry with me. I couldn't help it . . . I was on a case and I had to follow that

man . . . you know . . . the prestidigitator . . . he is the man I was investigating. I hope you're not mad at me.

CHRISTINE (off): Of course, I understand . . . no, no, not at all, I understand perfectly . . . I know what it means to be a detective . . .

ANTOINE: Yes . . . you say that, but I can hear that you're mad . . . I can understand that you would be a little angry . . .

CHRISTINE (off): No, I swear it . . . not at all. I mean it . . . you mustn't think that.

Across the way, people are passing in front of the post office.

ANTOINE (off): Listen . . . if you like . . . if you want to . . . we could go out tonight . . . or get together . . . or something! If you would, it would make me very happy.

CHRISTINE (off): I'd like it too, but I'm a little tired because I went to a demonstration last night . . .

ANTOINE: Oh, I see.

A rolling truck stops right in front of the post office.

ANTOINE: A demonstration? With the cops, the clubs, the beatings . . . all that stuff?

CHRISTINE (off): Yes, yes, yes.

Antoine is staring at the truck, which conceals the post office entrance from him.

ANTOINE: I get it.

CHRISTINE (off): Yes, you know my friend Marie-Aimée?

ANTOINE (nervously): I see . . . yes, that's very interesting.

CHRISTINE (off): She got beaten up and had to go to the hospital. They're really revolting, you know.

ANTOINE (growing increasingly nervous because of the truck): Oh, good.

CHRISTINE (off): So her father tried to file a complaint at the police station and they wouldn't even listen to him . . .
ANTOINE (trying to wind up the phone call): Good, very good . . . [To avoid hanging up on her, he knocks on the dial with a key and shouts into the receiver.] Hello, hello, mademoiselle . . . don't cut me off, operator . . . Hello, hello . . . Listen, Christine, I can't hear you anymore. There's too much noise on this line.
CHRISTINE (off): Hello, hello . . . what's going on here . . . what are those noises?
ANTOINE (still knocking): I can't hear you . . . too much noise.

As Antoine nervously hangs up, we see the truck moving off in the background. He rushes out of the booth, puts his cap on and paces back and forth, his eyes on the building across the way. A cop is making out a ticket for a car that is double-parked. A man in his thirties emerges from a bookstore and comes over to the car.

CAR OWNER: Hey, you. What do you think you're doing . . . putting that dirty paper on my windshield . . . [He walks around the car, takes the ticket off the windshield, and after looking at it, throws it away.] Messing up my car! That's dirty . . . on my car! [He gets into the car.] Those little pieces of paper are filthy!

Antoine, who has been following all of this, bursts into laughter . . . just as a post office employee begins to close the gates of the building. Antoine leaps over, hurries up the stairs, argues with the employee, but gets nowhere. Disappointed, he walks down the steps, looks at his watch, raises his eyes to heaven and walks backward until he runs into a sign reading "One-Way Street." He walks away.

BLADY'S OFFICE. INTERIOR. DAY.
Blady is seated at his desk studying some files.

BLADY (*reading a report*): Six-fifty-five, an employee of the post office locks up. Six-fifty-eight, there is still no sign of the subject.

A rear traveling shot now reveals the desk, with Antoine, his arms crossed, standing in front of it.

BLADY (*resumes his reading*): At seven-oh-four, I give up . . . If I read you correctly, it means that the prestidigitator spent all night locked inside the post office . . . is that it? You must be kidding!
ANTOINE: No, monsieur . . . but . . . he gave me the slip . . . I really can't imagine how.
BLADY: Of course, since he's a magician, he just made himself vanish into thin air, is that it? All right . . . what kind of a dive is this nightclub . . . is it a cabaret deluxe?
ANTOINE: No, monsieur, it's a rather arty place . . . with candles on the tables and Vivaldi music in . . . in the rest rooms.
BLADY: What about this statue you refer to here.
ANTOINE: Yes, that's right, he makes all his appointments out in the street . . . in front of a statue of Joan of Arc.
BLADY: An equestrian statue?
INTERPHONE VOICE: Monsieur Tabard is here for his appointment, sir.
BLADY: Show him in. [*To Antoine.*] Well, I'm absolutely certain that the . . . euh . . . magician spotted you, so I'll have to put someone else on the case. What am I going to do with you? Yes, I know you're full of good will, but you're discouraging.

Antoine, who has been listening in silence, looks down at his feet as Blady closes his file.

BLADY: Well, all right. That's all.

The door opens to let Antoine out as Catherine ushers a man into the office.

CATHERINE: Monsieur Tabard, sir.

Remaining outside, Catherine closes the door as Tabard, wearing a raincoat, steps over to Blady's desk.

TABARD: How do you do, sir. Tabard.
BLADY: Pleased to met you. Please sit down.

Tabard removes his coat and sits down as Blady, a pad in front of him and pencil in hand, prepares to take notes.

TABARD (off): I might as well tell you frankly . . . that I've got no particular reason for coming to see you.
BLADY: It's rather unusual for a person to come here out of sheer curiosity. But . . . Let's see . . . are you married, Monsieur Tabard?
TABARD: A wonderful marriage, yes . . . euh . . . with a superior-type woman, if I say so myself. No problems there at all. And I enjoy excellent health.
BLADY: I'm delighted to hear it. May I ask you what line of work you're in?
TABARD: Oh, the store is doing very well . . . very well indeed. Euh . . . we double our gross every season.
BLADY: What kind of store?
TABARD: Well . . . what kind of . . . My shoe shop. Shoes for men, women and children, children especially . . . Everybody needs shoes, isn't that so? . . . And with traffic the way it is, there are more and more pedestrians . . .
BLADY: Well, then, as I see it you are a happy man . . . a man with no worries . . . with no enemies . . .
TABARD: Hmm . . . with no enemies might be going too far . . . since my early childhood . . . in college, in the Army . . . people have been jealous of me. Mind you, it doesn't keep me from sleeping . . . besides, I have one serious weakness . . . I'm very frank.
BLADY: I agree . . . one can hurt people by being frank. But . . .

I'm not sure of the purpose of your visit . . . Just what do you expect of me?

TABARD: Well, you see . . . The point is nobody likes me and I want to find out why that is . . . Yes, I know what you're about to say: Why don't I see a psychiatrist? Right? It's not the money, believe me, I can afford it. But I don't want to waste my time telling the story of my life on somebody's couch. I'm not a sissy, you know . . . Besides, my shop keeps me very busy. A bootmaker works twenty-four hours a day, or else he should be in another line of work . . . that's what I say!

BLADY: I see, but if you think that everybody hates you, isn't it just possible that you tend to look down on people?

TABARD: Oh, no. Never . . . absolutely not. I don't despise anybody. You know anyone can get their shoes at Tabard's . . . I sell shoes to Jewish women . . . to Arabs . . . and even to Chinks . . . on the condition, of course, that they're willing to wear high heels . . . Hah! That'll be the day! No . . . I feel that I'm hated and I don't know by whom . . . I simply don't know . . . but I feel it in the air . . . when I go out . . . to a restaurant . . . to the movies . . . when I go to a prize fight. I'm not sure my concierge hates me, but it's a fact that whenever I speak to her, she shrugs her shoulders . . . and my wife's always laughing at me . . . except when I tell her a funny story . . . Then there are the salesgirls . . . they're the worst . . . Whenever I make a comment on their work, they talk back . . . they argue . . . they quibble.

BLADY: You've got friends, haven't you?

TABARD: Euh . . . no . . . not a single one. No friends. Mind you, I don't need any . . . which is just as well, because if I needed them, I wouldn't know where to look!

BLADY: How many salesgirls do you have?

TABARD: Four, plus the cashier.

BLADY: Well now, suppose we start by looking into your shop. I might put a periscope in there.

TABARD: What do you mean?

BLADY: Euh . . . yes, a periscope. I'll explain it to you . . .

DETECTIVES' OFFICE IN THE BLADY AGENCY.
INTERIOR. DAY.
Paul and Antoine are working out a puzzle in the newspaper.
In the background we see Henri, Catherine, and Ida, the secretary,
who is typing something.

INTERPHONE (*Blady's voice*): Send Doinel in, please.
IDA: Yes, sir, right away. Antoine, Monsieur Blady wants to see you.

Antoine, intent on his puzzle, fails to respond.

IDA: He said right away!
ANTOINE (*to Paul*): Here goes . . . I'm getting hell again!

As he walks across the office, he passes Henri.

HENRI: I can only tell you what my father told me the day I left
to come to Paris: Be deferential to your superiors!

BLADY'S OFFICE. INTERIOR. DAY.
Antoine heads for Blady's office.

BLADY (*off*): Here's the periscope!

Antoine looks up, startled.

BLADY: Monsieur Tabard, let me introduce Antoine Doinel.
Antoine Doinel, this is Monsieur Tabard.
ANTOINE: How do you do.
BLADY: All right. You may go now, Doinel.

Antoine walks out of the room, leaving the two men together.

TABARD: He's young.
BLADY: Yes, but he's brilliant . . . . especially on an investigation
. . . [*with a sigh*] though as a shadower, he leaves something to be
desired . . .
TABARD: All right. Let him report on Monday morning and I'll
hire him . . .
BLADY: Oh no, that would be foolish . . . they would understand
right away that he's your man. It'd be best if they thought you
didn't know him. What you'll do is place a want ad in *France-Soir*:
"Stock Boy Wanted." Then you eliminate the others and you hire
him.
TABARD: Fine.

TABARD SHOE STORE. INTERIOR. DAY.
In the back room of the store five young men are standing
behind two trestles on which there are shoe boxes and wrapping
paper. Antoine is among them. Tabard walks back and forth,
rubbing his hands together.

TABARD: When I give the signal, you start . . . right? [*Checking
his watch.*] Ready . . . one . . . two . . . three . . . go!

The five boys get to work on their packages. A close-up on the
first box and the hands of the young man who is competently folding
the paper around it. A shot of the second box, already in its wrapping, and on the third, which Antoine is fumbling with. The fourth
and fifth boxes are perfectly wrapped up. Tabard walks behind
them, inspecting their work. While all the others have passed the
test with flying colors, Antoine hasn't even managed to tie a string
around his box.

TABARD: All right, now present your packages.

Antoine lifts his half-finished package. Tabard taps him on the shoulder.

TABARD (*heartily to Antoine*): That's splendid, just splendid. We'll hire this one. [*Antoine looks embarrassed.*] A good job, very good! [*Antoine lifts his head and beams proudly.*]

A STAIRWAY STREET IN MONTMARTRE.
EXTERIOR. DAY.

A young man, wearing his hair very long, is coming down the stairs of a Montmartre street. He stops at one of the landings to search through a municipal trash can containing old papers and garbage. He picks up a newspaper, puts it in his briefcase, peers into the trash can again, then puts the lid back on and proceeds down the staircase. He passes Antoine going up, pretends not to see him, then has second thoughts.

YOUNG MAN: Hi, there! [*They shake hands.*]
ANTOINE: Hi. How are things?
YOUNG MAN: How are you?
ANTOINE: Fine . . . euh . . . I work in a shoe store now.
YOUNG MAN: Oh, well . . . things are all right with me too. You know my television scripts . . .
ANTOINE: Yes?
YOUNG MAN: I took them to one of the channels. They read them . . . they liked them very much . . . they're interested. I'm waiting . . . but they'll produce them . . . that's for sure . . .
ANTOINE: Oh, great, great.
YOUNG MAN: So I'm pleased.
ANTOINE (*hastily*): Good, good, good. Well, so long!

They shake hands. The young man goes down and Antoine walks up.

Young Man: G'bye now.
Antoine: So long.

TABARD SHOE STORE. INTERIOR. DAY.

Antoine comes into the stock room carrying two high stacks of shoe boxes in his arms. In the background we see the shop. The cashier is at her desk and a salesgirl is trying some shoes on a customer. Tabard is arranging some publicity balloons for children in the entrance. Antoine, wearing a gray smock, takes some of the boxes over to the cashier's desk and goes back to the stock room. As Antoine removes his smock, a salesgirl walks over to him.

Antoine: Say, is there . . . is there a restaurant around here?
Marianne: Oh, don't go out for lunch. Eat here with us.
Antoine: How does it work?
Marianne: Well, most of the time we share . . . we bring things and share them.
Antoine: I'm afraid I'd be in your way.

Another salesgirl, Sophie, walks in and presses Antoine to join them in the rear of the store.

Sophie: Never mind, just stay with us. We'll manage. [*They enter a tiny alcove crowded with stacks of shoes.*] Come and help me set the table.
Antoine: Say . . . the owner . . . euh . . . Monsieur Tabard . . . I think he's a good guy . . .
Sophie (*bubbling with laughter*): It's obvious you don't know him: he's a dinosaur!

Late afternoon, the salesgirls are getting into their coats on their way out. As Antoine is removing his smock, Mme. Turgan bursts into the stock room and addresses him in a harsh tone of voice.

MME. TURGAN: You're not leaving till you locate that pair of Louis Fifteenth pumps I asked for . . .
ANTOINE: Look, madame, they're not here. I've gone through all my slips . . . they never came in . . .

The two of them step aside to make way for the salesladies on their way out.

MME. TURGAN: My dear boy, you obviously have a great deal to learn . . .
A SALESGIRL: Good night, Madame Turgan.
MME. TURGAN: The factory double-checked it for me. That delivery was made . . . in fact you signed the delivery slip.

Another salesgirl passes them on the way out. Mme. Turgan ignores her "good night," while Antoine fumbles with the boxes.

ANTOINE: But . . . I sign lots of delivery slips and papers . . . I've been signing all day . . . I don't know where those shoes are . . . I've looked everywhere . . .
MME. TURGAN: Well, they're here . . . someplace . . . somebody must have switched the boxes . . . Go through the whole store . . . strip the shelves if necessary. I don't care how you do it, but I need those shoes first thing tomorrow morning.

She walks out stiffly, while Antoine puts his jacket down and reluctantly walks over to the stack ladder. At the top rung of the ladder he turns around and sits down with his legs stretched out to the stacks across the aisle. After a while Antoine comes down and keeps on searching. Suddenly he hears something that makes him stop. He walks silently into the store. Here we discover a lovely woman, elegantly dressed in a long black dress and a white silk scarf; she is nonchalantly selecting a pair of shoes from the window display. Antoine is stupefied.

ANTOINE: Madame, you can't just come in here like this.

The woman turns around in surprise . . . but in the same nonchalant way picks up a second shoe from the showcase, takes off one of her own, throws it on the floor and calmly sits down to try on the slipper of her choice.

ANTOINE: The store is closed. What if all the customers did that?
THE WOMAN (smiling): Well, if all the customers did what I do, they would all be Fabienne Tabard, I suppose . . . I am the boss's wife.
ANTOINE: Oh . . . excuse me . . . I'm really . . . This is embarrassing . . . I'm really sorry . . .
FABIENNE: It doesn't matter in the least . . . you're just doing your job. Are you the new boy?
ANTOINE: Yes, I am, yes.
FABIENNE: Antoine, isn't that right? What do you think of these shoes?

She has got a shoe in her hand and is studying it. Antoine is too intimidated to speak.

FABIENNE (off): Too golden for this dress, huh? You're absolutely right. Let's try something else. Find me a pair of sandals like these [Antoine is enthralled by this apparition.] . . . but with black satin tips. Size four and a half . . . all right?
ANTOINE: Yes!

He rushes back to the stock room, stealing a few furtive glances at Fabienne. He emerges with a box in his hand, comes over to her, opens the box and hands her a shoe. We hear the sound of a car horn honking in the street.

FABIENNE (sighing): Monsieur Tabard is impatient for a change

. . . [*She tries the shoes on. The telephone rings.*] Oh, will you take it, please?

Antoine walks to the desk and picks up the receiver.

ANTOINE: Hello . . .
VOICE (*off*): May I speak to Mrs. Tabard?*
ANTOINE (*awkwardly*): What . . . I don't understand you . . .

Fabienne comes over and hands Antoine a box with her old shoes in it.

ANTOINE: I don't speak . . . euh . . . one moment. [*To Fabienne.*] It's in English. I don't understand a word.

Antoine steps aside and stares in awe as Fabienne picks up the receiver.

FABIENNE: Hello, Dick . . . Yes, I know I'm late.† I'm sorry. Yes, well, you go ahead. We'll join you later. I'm still at the store. Right. Tell Jeannette I'm sorry . . . Georges is waiting outside. Good-bye!

As she hangs up, Antoine hands her the box containing her shoes, but she waves it aside.

FABIENNE: Do you mind taking that up to the apartment? You can go up now. I've got to rush. Good night, Antoine! [*She opens the door.*] You know how to lock up? [*He nods affirmatively.*] You're working very late, aren't you?

With a final smile, she walks out. Antoine watches through

* In the script this sentence is in English.
† In the film, Fabienne's whole phone conversation is in English.

the window as she gets into Tabard's car, which moves off. He goes over to the door to lock up for the night.

DETECTIVES' OFFICE IN THE BLADY AGENCY.
INTERIOR. NIGHT.
Ida, the secretary, is typing at her desk. The phone rings.

IDA: Hello . . . yes?

PUBLIC TELEPHONE BOOTH. STREET.
EXTERIOR. NIGHT.
Antoine is at the other end of the wire.

ANTOINE: Hello, Ida. This is Antoine.
IDA (off): Hi, Antoine, how are things?
ANTOINE: Well, the personnel refers to Monsieur Tabard as the dinosaur . . . [He checks his notebook.] Oh, yes, I just met Madame Tabard. She has an enchanting voice and her English is absolutely flawless.
IDA (businesslike and off): Give me her description.
ANTOINE (very emphatic): She's a fabulous woman! She seems a little vague and is very gentle. Her nose is straight and witty . . . and the tip is slightly turned up . . .
IDA (off): Her dimensions?
ANTOINE: She has a very slender waist.
IDA (briskly, off): I'm asking how tall she is?
ANTOINE: Oh . . . about five foot five . . . without heels.
IDA (off): What shape face?
ANTOINE (waxing lyrical): It's a perfect oval shape . . . I mean a slightly triangular oval. And her complexion is radiant . . . as if illuminated from within!

DETECTIVES' OFFICE IN THE BLADY AGENCY.
INTERIOR. NIGHT.

By now Ida is very irritated.

IDA: Look, Antoine. What we want is a report, not a declaration of love! Good night! [*She hangs up on him.*]

PUBLIC TELEPHONE BOOTH. STREET. EXTERIOR.
NIGHT.

Antoine is visibly put out as he too hangs up.

ANTOINE'S ROOM. INTERIOR. DAY.

Antoine, in his pajamas, is shaving. His face covered with lather, he is listening to a voice speaking English.

VOICE (*off*): Does your friend speak English?
ANTOINE (*laboriously replies*): No, my friend doesn't speak English.
VOICE (*off*): He understands it, but he doesn't speak it.
ANTOINE (*repeating*): He understands it, but he doesn't speak it.
VOICE (*off*): I don't pronounce it very well.
ANTOINE (*repeating*): I don't pronounce it very well.

Throughout this strange dialogue a pan around the room shows the unmade bed; then the camera moves down to show a record spinning on a pickup and next to it the red jackets of the English Course records.

PICKUP: Do you understand me?
ANTOINE (*off*): Do you understand me?
PICKUP: Oh, yes, but you need practice. How do you spell that word?

STREET. TABARD SHOE STORE. EXTERIOR. DAY.

Christine walks slowly in front of the store, hesitates in front of the door and looks in through the window. Inside are two salesgirls, a few customers, the cashier and Fabienne Tabard. Finally Christine makes up her mind and walks in. The camera remains outside and the following scene is seen through the store windows.

A salesgirl approaches Christine, who asks her a question. Then Fabienne Tabard walks up to her and moves off with a smile. Going up to one of the salesgirls, she says something to her while looking over at Christine. A customer, with two little children, each wearing a Laurel and Hardy mask, leaves the store. Antoine, looking rather embarrassed, appears in the background and goes over to Christine. The two of them talk together, then he leads her to the door and they both leave.

AVENUE. EXTERIOR. DAY.

Antoine and Christine are strolling side by side along an avenue lined with tall trees. Antoine sounds irritated.

ANTOINE: How could you come barging in the store right in the middle of the working day . . .
CHRISTINE: Well, we never hear from you and you're never home. My parents were wondering what happened to you.
ANTOINE (*still irritated*): You just tell them that I'm perfectly all right and give them my best regards.
CHRISTINE: You can be awfully unpleasant at times . . . with no reason.
ANTOINE: Sure . . . no reason . . . no reason at all.
CHRISTINE: If you've got a reason, why don't you tell me what it is?
ANTOINE: Oh, nothing . . . nothing at all!
CHRISTINE: I thought I was your friend.
ANTOINE: Look, just save your friendship for a rainy day . . . or spread it around . . . but me . . .
CHRISTINE: We're right back to where we were last year.

Still walking and facing the camera, their voices are rising.

ANTOINE: No, not back to where we were . . . we're much farther behind than that. And you know who's to blame!
CHRISTINE: It's certainly not my fault. I can't remember all your letters, but once you wrote me. "Now I know that what I feel for you is purely a deep friendship." Didn't you write me something like that? Now be honest!
ANTOINE: Yes, that's true . . . I thought so at the time . . . but you know that love and friendship go hand in hand with admiration. Well, even when I thought I loved you, I didn't admire you. And that's the truth!
CHRISTINE (vexed): Very well, then. Good-bye!

Angrily, both of them walk off in different directions. A panoramic shot of the alley reveals the strange man in the trench coat following Christine as she disappears in the distance.

TABARD SHOE STORE. INTERIOR. DAY.
Two salesgirls, Françoise and Marianne, are in the stock room. One of them is perched on a low ladder; the other one is blowing up a small publicity balloon, which bursts.

MARIANNE: Hey, look at Papa Tabard!

The two girls are unaware that Fabienne Tabard has emerged from the basement and is listening to their conversation.

FRANÇOISE (off): I hate to go there by myself!
MARIANNE (off): Well, why don't you ask the new boy to go with you?
FRANÇOISE (off): Antoine?

The camera goes back to the two salesladies.

MARIANNE: Yeah, Antoine's not so bad. I wouldn't mind making it with him.

Fabienne listens with a slight smile.

FRANÇOISE (off): Yes, he's okay . . . but haven't you noticed? He's crazy about the boss's wife.
MARIANNE (off): Madame Tabard?
FRANÇOISE (off): In person! The other day Sylvie was kidding around and she said: "Here comes Madame Dinosaur." Antoine flew into a rage. "Aren't you ashamed of yourselves . . . talking that way about such a remarkable woman." He really carried on! He said: "Madame Tabard is not a woman, she's an apparition!" MARIANNE (in surprise): He said she's an apparition?

Back to Fabienne, who has a slightly ironic smile and looks delighted.

FRANÇOISE: You heard me right: he said an apparition! Haven't you noticed that whenever she walks in he turns as white as a sheet!

ANTOINE'S ROOM. INTERIOR. DAY.
Antoine, still in his pajamas, is looking into the mirror above the sink. Staring at his image, he repeats the name of Fabienne Tabard over and over again in a passionate tone of voice.

ANTOINE: Fabienne Tabard, Fabienne Tabard, Fabienne Tabard, Fabienne Tabard, Fabienne Tabard, Fabienne Tabard . . .

The rhyme of this repetition accelerates and finally dissolves into the name of Christine.

ANTOINE: Christine Darbon, Christine Darbon, Christine Darbon, Christine Darbon, Christine Darbon, Christine Darbon . . .

Eventually he slows down and gestures with his hand to lower the tone. He stops, then goes back to the name of Fabienne Tabard with his own name, speaking very slowly, with one hand held up facing the mirror.

ANTOINE: Fabienne Tabard, Antoine Doinel, Fabienne Tabard, Antoine Doinel, Antoine Doinel, Antoine Doinel . . . [*His voice grows louder as he stresses the "toi" and "doi" of his name.*] AnTOIne DOInel . . . [*When he is out of breath, he rubs his face and splashes some water over it.*]

TABARD SHOE STORE. INTERIOR. DAY.

Marianne is looking for a box in the stock room when Tabard appears.

TABARD: No, not on that shelf. Look up there . . . in those green boxes.

Marianne draws the stepladder over, but before going up, she turns to Tabard.

MARIANNE: Those boxes are empty!
TABARD (*unruffled*): The green boxes!

Before complying, Marianne makes a gesture indicating that her boss is nuts. As she goes slowly up the stepladder, Tabard stands right beneath her, looking up at her legs. Marianne opens a green box and shows him that it is empty.

MARIANNE: Monsieur Tabard, can I have my day off tomorrow?
TABARD (*curtly*): No!
MARIANNE: Would you like to hear a story?

She comes down, holding the green box. The two face each other.

TABARD: No!
MARIANNE (*ironically*): You know the one about the idiot who always says no?
TABARD: No!
MARIANNE: You said it . . . I didn't!

Antoine, concealed behind the stacks, laughs appreciatively.

ANTOINE (*to himself*): Oh, brother!

Tabard goes over to him and whispers.

TABARD: Come with me. [*The two of them walk out.*]

HALLWAY OF THE BUILDING. INTERIOR. DAY.
　　Tabard and Antoine are heading for the elevator.

TABARD (*sighing*): You heard that, didn't you? It's like that all the time. [*They go into the elevator.*] How's the investigation going? Have you any new leads?
ANTOINE (*assuming his professional manner*): I'm not at liberty to say. I make my report every evening and Monsieur Blady draws the conclusions, but if you want some additional information . . .

THE TABARD APARTMENT. INTERIOR. DAY.
　　Close-up of a very handsome mirror with a gilded carved frame, which reflects the elevator door inside the apartment. Antoine and Tabard get out and cross the foyer. Tabard picks up some book-keeping ledgers and heads for the dining room. Stealing furtive glances at the elegant decor, Antoine follows him.

TABARD: And who do you suppose made this year's largest contribution to the Protective Association for Shoemen? Yours truly, that's who!
ANTOINE: I see.

　　The two men move over toward the table where Fabienne is already eating. Antoine stands politely at one end of the table, while Tabard puts the ledgers down on the sideboard and sits down.

FABIENNE: Really, Georges, where were you? Everything's cold . . . shall I have it warmed up?
TABARD: No, don't bother, I'll eat on the run. Is there any cheese? That will be fine. I was stuck downstairs . . . the girls got the boxes all mixed up.

FABIENNE (*looking at Antoine*): Hello, Antoine.

Antoine walks over to her and timidly looking down shakes her hand.

ANTOINE: Good afternoon.
TABARD (*off*): I've got to give the ledgers to Antoine.
FABIENNE (*to Antoine*): Have you had your lunch?
ANTOINE: Euh, yes . . . downstairs.
FABIENNE: With the girls?
ANTOINE: That's right, with the girls.

Tabard motions to Antoine to sit down at the table, across from Fabienne.

TABARD: One of the books is missing. I'll give it to you later.

Fabienne, smiling, looks straight at Antoine, while Tabard hands him a plate.

ANTOINE: Thank you.

Fabienne is still staring at Antoine.

TABARD (*off*): Do you like cheese? This one's perfect. It has a wonderful stink.
ANTOINE: Euh . . . I'd really prefer a yogurt, please.

Antoine looks toward Fabienne, who picks up a yogurt and hands it to him, smiling. He thanks her with a nod of the head.

FABIENNE: Dick and Jeannette called. I told them to call you in the store.
TABARD: Yes, I called back too late. They were already at Berlitz for their first French lesson. Antoine, do you speak English?

ANTOINE: Euh . . . I'm trying to learn with records, but it's pretty tough.

TABARD: Records are a waste of time. There's only one way to do it . . . you study in bed with an English girl. You should really do something about it. I learned English that way with an Australian girl while her husband was at work. He was a house painter.

FABIENNE: (*daintily wiping her mouth with her napkin*): Like Hitler!

TABARD (*remonstrating*): You should never say that Hitler was a house painter. That's slander! Hitler was a little landscape painter.

Fabienne smiles, while Antoine is not quite sure how to react. Tabard stands up. Antoine digs into his yogurt. Tabard, still looking for his missing ledger, suddenly strikes his head.

TABARD: What am I thinking about! Of course, the ledger is in the car. I'll run down and get it. Wait here, Antoine, I'll be right back.

A servant walks in with the coffee tray. Fabienne takes it from her and puts it down on a coffee table in the living room.

FABIENNE: Let it go. I'll serve it myself. [*Turning back to Antoine.*] Come on.

Antoine settles down on the couch, facing her. She hands him a cup and pours coffee into it, then hands him the sugar bowl. He takes one lump and as she is about to put the sugar bowl down he holds it back.

ANTOINE: I'll have another one if I may.

She smiles and he responds to her smile. She pours some coffee for herself. Stirring it, she looks at him, very much at ease. Unable to meet her eyes, he looks down in embarrassment. After a few minutes, she gets up and goes over to the turntable gramophone. He

stares at her, fascinated. She turns her back on him to look for a record; he takes advantage of it to spoon his coffee into his mouth. She finds the record and leans down to put it on the pickup.

FABIENNE: Do you like music, Antoine?
ANTOINE (*stares at her distractedly*): Yes, sir!

A close-up of Antoine as he realizes his blunder. He is petrified! Reverse shot of Fabienne as she looks up in astonishment. A quick cut on the cup he has spilled followed by a panoramic shot showing his flight as he jumps up and rushes toward the door.

STAIRWAY. INTERIOR. DAY.

Antoine hurries down the stairs, with the camera following his descent. At the ground floor he stops to wipe the sweat off his brow and heads for the door leading into the stock room.

TABARD SHOE STORE. INTERIOR. DAY.

Inside the stock room Antoine scurries through the shoe stacks. Françoise, perched on a stepladder, looks at him in surprise.

FRANÇOISE: Hey, Antoine, what's going on?

Ignoring her, he bolts over to the checkroom, grabs his coat and puts it on.

ANTOINE: I'm not working this afternoon. I'm sick. I'm going home.

He dashes through the shoe store. As he's opening the door, Mme. Turgan, the manageress, calls out to him.

MME. TURGAN: Antoine! Where are you going?
ANTOINE: I'm sick. I'm going home. [*He closes the door behind him and goes off.*]

Fabienne, wearing a suit and carrying a purse, opens the door leading to the stock room and weaves in and out of the stacks and rows of shoe boxes, apparently looking for someone. After a while she steps into the shop and questions Françoise.

FABIENNE: That new stock-room boy . . . [*She seems to be search-ing for his name.*] . . . Antoine . . . Do you know where he is?
FRANÇOISE: He's gone home. He wasn't feeling well.

Fabienne marches over to Mme. Turgan at the cash register.

FABIENNE: May I see the book, please . . . [*Mme. Turgan hands her a ledger.*] No! . . . the address book! [*Fabienne takes it and after looking up Antoine's address, repeats it to herself as she hands the book back to Mme. Turgan.*] Thank you.

In the background a customer is trying on a pair of shoes and examining them in the foot mirrors. Fabienne leaves the store. A pan reveals Catherine of the Blady Agency following Fabienne at a discreet distance.

THE BLADY AGENCY. INTERIOR. DAY.

Albani, a customer, is sitting in the corridor waiting to speak to Blady. Antoine hurries past him to go into the detective's office. After removing his coat he begins to pace up and down. Henri is at his desk writing up a report.

HENRI: Say, is there some word I can use instead of "said"? I've al-ready used it ten times in this report . . . it doesn't sound right.
IDA: You can use "confided," "revealed," "related," "claimed" . . .
HENRI: You sure know all about words, don't you? On second thought, I think I'll stick to "said" . . . it looks better.

Ida and Henri pay no attention to Antoine, who is hanging up his coat. Catherine walks in exhausted, drops into a chair near the door and kicks off her shoes:

CATHERINE: That beautiful Madame Tabard . . . she sure had me on the run . . . But at last I've got a lead now!

ANTOINE: A lead . . . what lead?
CATHERINE (*sounding confident*): On her lover, of course!

Antoine is visibly upset by the announcement. Nervously pacing back and forth, he sounds outraged.

ANTOINE: Madame Tabard has no lover! She's way above that sort of thing!
CATHERINE: Is that so? Just one half hour ago she went into Cardinus and bought three long neckties. Her husband never wears them.

ANTOINE (*thoughtfully*): You're right. He only wears bow ties . . . [*Suddenly he explodes.*] I'm fed up with that case! I'm going to ask Monsieur Blady to assign me to something else.

He crosses the hall and knocks at the door of Blady's office.

BLADY (*off*): Yes?

Antoine walks in, leaving the door open.

ANTOINE: Excuse me for interrupting you, but I have to speak to you about something important.

Blady gets up and ushers Antoine into the hall, where both of them speak at the same time, with Blady ignoring Antoine.

BLADY (*busily*): Not right now. I've got to see Monsieur Albani first.
ANTOINE: But it's urgent I see you now. Please . . . it will only take a few minutes.
BLADY: Now, really! Listen to me. You can wait for five minutes, can't you? Have a little patience.
ANTOINE: It's truly a very urgent matter.

Blady steps over to Albani.

BLADY: Monsieur Albani . . .

He points to his office. Antoine persists and follows Blady, pleading with him.

ANTOINE: Look, I won't take very long. Just give me two minutes of your time, please!
BLADY: I will see you in a little while.

He goes into his office, closing the door behind him. Disappointed, Antoine slowly goes back to the detectives' office and sits down at Henri's desk.

HENRI: How are things?

BLADY'S OFFICE. INTERIOR. DAY.
Albani, facing the camera (and Blady's desk), is all ears.

BLADY (off): Well, we were pretty lucky in your case. We're not always successful, you know. Anyway, we shadowed your friend, the prestidigitator.
ALBANI: Robert . . .
BLADY: That's right [reading from his file] . . . Monsieur Robert Espanet. Thirty-five years old. It says here that he's been doing a prestidigitation act at Le Cheval d'Or since last September. [Blady looks over at Albani's hands.] Let's see . . . he is currently residing at 42 Avenue de la République. [Blady looks up as Albani repeats the address to himself in order to memorize it.] He needs more room because his wife is expecting a baby.
ALBANI (incredulous): His wife?
BLADY: Yes, he was married on November twelfth.
ALBANI: You must be mistaken!
BLADY: Not at all. I have all the details here: the marriage contract was drawn up by a notary—Maître Lebaudet!

Albani, who has been listening attentively, becomes very agitated. He stands up in a rage.

ALBANI (screaming): You are a shyster, monsieur! You're lying!

Albani grabs the file and begins to tear it to pieces. Blady tries to get it back from him.

BLADY: Monsieur, please! Give me back those papers!
ALBANI (*still screaming*): You are an unprincipled liar!
BLADY: Let me have those papers!

Albani wildly tries to hit Blady.

ALBANI: There's not a word of truth! It's blackmail! It's all a pack of filthy lies!

Blady tries to pull away from him.

BLADY: Just give me back that file and calm down. Take it easy, now!

Albani stamps on the floor and hits Blady.

ALBANI: You dirty louse! You lousy bastard!

Blady manages to pin Albani against the wall.

BLADY: Take it easy . . . please!
ALBANI: Don't touch me!

Antoine, Catherine and Henri rush in and try to hold onto Albani, who has gone berserk.

HENRI: Good God . . . what's going on here . . . they've gone mad! Catherine, run upstairs and get the dentist down here. [*To Albani.*] Come on now, calm down!

Catherine runs out of the office.

THE LANDING OF THE BLADY BUILDING.
INTERIOR. DAY.

On the floor above, the sign on the door indicates that it is a dentist's office. Catherine rings; the door is opened by the dentist's assistant. Catherine rushes in. The dentist is working on a patient in the background.

CATHERINE: Josette, quick, quick! The doctor!
JOSETTE: I can't let you in now . . . it's impossible!

Catherine pushes her out of the way.

CATHERINE: I'm sorry . . . [*She grabs the dentist by the arm.*] Doctor, quickly, quickly . . . there's a madman in the agency!
DENTIST (*to his client*): Excuse me!

Catherine and the dentist go out to the hall and bolt down the stairs.

BLADY'S OFFICE. INTERIOR. DAY.

Albani is still fighting, hitting out and shrieking hysterically at Blady.

ALBANI: Let me go, you son of a bitch! Don't touch me, you bastard!
HENRI: (*soothingly*): There, there . . .

The dentist comes in, walks up to Albani, grabs him and gives him two hard slaps that immediately calm him down.

CATHERINE: We must take him home.

All the fight has now gone out of Albani; he is almost sobbing as the dentist helps him toward the door. Antoine steps aside to let them pass.

ALBANI (crying): No, I don't want to go home. He left all his things there. I never want to see him again.

HALLWAY OF THE BLADY AGENCY. INTERIOR. DAY.
Catherine urges Albani over to the door.

CATHERINE: You've got to go someplace.
ALBANI: I'll go to a hotel.
HENRI: Put him in a cab and take him home. Go on.

Albani and Catherine leave. Antoine and Blady go back into the office as Henri stands at the door, holding it open.

HENRI (to Blady): What was the point of all that? I suppose you're proud of yourself. [He closes the door.] Anyway, I hope he paid in advance!

ANTOINE'S BUILDING. INTERIOR. EVENING.
As Antoine is walking up the stairs the lights go out. When he reaches his own floor he turns the light on again, takes his keys out and then looks down in surprise. He picks up a gift package with a letter on top of it. Rising slowly, he reads the name on the envelope and leans against the wall to read the note, which is from Fabienne Tabard.

FABIENNE'S VOICE (off): When I was at college, one of my professors explained to us the difference between tact and courtesy. A gentleman house guest accidentally pushes the bathroom door open to find himself in front of a lady who's stark naked. He withdraws at once and, as he's closing the door, he says: "I beg your pardon, madame!" That is courtesy! When the same man pushes the door open and, discovering the same stark-naked lady, says: "Oh, I beg your pardon, monsieur!" that is tact! I understood your flight, Antoine. Till tomorrow!

ANTOINE'S ROOM. INTERIOR. EVENING.

Seated at the table, Antoine is writing a letter. We see only his hands in front of the paper and next to his hands, the open package containing three ties.

ANTOINE (inner voice): Madame . . . I have been looking at these ties, which I would never dare to wear . . .

He tears the sheet off the note pad, crumples it, throws it away and starts on a new page.

ANTOINE (inner voice): This is a letter of farewell. You are magnanimous and I am unworthy of your generosity. You will never see me again. I am not going back to the store; I am handing in my resignation . . .

A PARIS STREET. EXTERIOR. NIGHT.

Antoine is walking along the street.

ANTOINE (inner voice): I am an impostor far beyond anything you would imagine. For a while I dreamed that something might happen between us . . . [Antoine passes a letter box to move over to an-

*other one marked "Pneumatique."**] . . . but that dream will die from the same impossibility that marked the love of Felix de Vandenesse for Madame de Mortsauf in The Lily of the Valley. Adieu. [After throwing the letter into the Pneumatique box he moves on.]*

PNEUMATIQUE DOCUMENTARY.

This sequence is a montage of shots illustrating the itinerary of a Pneumatique letter.

A close-up on Antoine's hand dropping the letter into the box. Inside, it is immediately picked up and turned over to another hand that puts it on a table, where it is rubber-stamped. The hand places the letter inside a metal roll and puts the roll into a suction tube leading to an underground pipeline that runs along the Paris sewerage system. We follow the course of the letter via a series of street indications: From the Rue Lepic to the Place Clichy, then the Rue Saint-Lazare, Rue La Fayette, Rue de la Boetie, Rue Richelieu, Avenue des Champs Elysées, Rue de la Paix, Rue de Rivoli and finally Avenue de l'Opéra. Eventually the metal roll drops into a basket. A hand picks it up and extracts the letter from the roll.

THE TABARD APARTMENT. INTERIOR. EARLY MORNING.

Fabienne's hands as she opens the Pneumatique letter.

RUE DE MONTMARTRE. EXTERIOR. EARLY MORNING.

A master shot of the Sacré-Coeur pans to the Rue de Montmartre. A sanitation department truck is spraying the street. A traveling shot toward the facade of a building gradually closes in on Antoine's window.

* In Paris, a letter mailed by Pneumatique will reach its destination within an hour or two. The following sequence is a graphic illustration of how the Pneumatique post office works.

ANTOINE'S ROOM. INTERIOR. EARLY MORNING.

Antoine is asleep in bed. There is a knock at the door. He wakes up with a start.

ANTOINE: What is it?

His pajamas are hanging on a rack next to the bed.

FABIENNE (off): Hush!

The door opens on a smiling Fabienne. Antoine can hardly believe his eyes as he pulls the blankets up to his nose. Fabienne walks in.

FABIENNE: Good morning, Antoine. Did I wake you? Well, I too was awakened early this morning by your Pneumatique, but I didn't mind a bit. It's very pleasant to wake up in the morning to read something so lovely. I was about to write a reply . . . and then I realized that I had to come here myself. [*Fabienne walks around the room.*] Look . . . I've read *The Lily of the Valley*, and like you, I think it's very beautiful. But you overlook one thing and that is that Madame de Mortsauf loved Felix de Vandenesse. It is not a beautiful love story . . . it is a pathetic tale . . . because in the end what caused her death was that she couldn't share that love with him [*She leans against the wall.*] Moreover, I am not an apparition, I am a woman . . . which is exactly the opposite! For instance, before coming here this morning, I put my make-up on. I powdered my nose, then I did my eyes . . .

Antoine lifts himself on one elbow in order to see her better.

FABIENNE: On my way here I noticed that all women do exactly the same thing . . . for their own pleasure or out of regard for others. You say that I am exceptional. That's true, I am exceptional. But then, every woman is exceptional . . . each in her own way.

You over there, you are certainly exceptional . . . Your fingerprints are the only ones of their kind in the whole world. Did you know that? You are unique. We are, each of us, unique . . . unique and irreplaceable.

She moves over to the window, looks out and turns back to lean against the wall. Next to her is a portrait of Jacques Audiberti* and a Balthus reproduction.

FABIENNE: Before he died, my father motioned to his doctor to come closer. He whispered to him: "People are wonderful" and died a few minutes later . . . I understand that you have nothing to say, but I want you to look at me . . . really look at me! You wrote me a letter last night. The answer is: me! [She moves over to the bed to look at Antoine.] I propose a contract that is fair to each of us. Since both of us like the exceptional, here it is: I'll come over there, by your side, now. We will spend a few hours together and then, no matter what happens, we will never see each other again. All right?
ANTOINE: Yes, yes, yes! [He smiles self-consciously as she slowly moves over to lock the door.]
FABIENNE: Maybe I should take the key out of the lock. In the novels we both like, the woman would take the key and throw it out of the window, but for us this vase should be fine. [She drops the key into the vase.]

HALLWAY OF ANTOINE'S BUILDING. INTERIOR. DAY.
Christine comes up the stairs and goes over to Antoine's door. There is no answer to her knock. After a while she tries the knob,

* Jacques Audiberti is a contemporary author and playwright who died in 1965.

but the door is locked. Disappointed, she turns back and goes downstairs.

RUE DES BUTTE-MONTMARTRE. EXTERIOR. DAY.

A master shot of the Sacré-Coeur in Montmartre. We pan down to show Christine walking along the street. We notice that she is being followed by the strange man in the trench coat; then a third person apears on the screen. It is Catherine, who is stationed in front of Antoine's building, watching the doorway.

THE BLADY AGENCY. INTERIOR. DAY.

Blady is at his desk. In a corner, Ida is taking notes, while Catherine, standing in front of the desk, is delivering her report. On the other side of the room, Paul and another operative are leafing through some files.

CATHERINE: And then this morning, a surprise: Madame Tabard, who never gets up before eleven, went out at eight-fifteen. I followed her over to 18 Square d'Anvers. She remained there a good hour and a half, then came down and went home.
BLADY: Do you know whom she visited there?
CATHERINE: No, it's an eight-story apartment building. The concierge wasn't in, but I intend to go back to speak to some of the tenants.

Only now do we notice that Antoine too is in the room. As he moves over to the desk, Catherine steps aside, looking a little surprised.

ANTOINE: Well, I know whom Madam Tabard was with.
BLADY (all ears): Yes? Who?

ANTOINE (*in a whisper*): Monsieur Blady . . . I'd like to have a word with you in private.

BLADY (*to the others*): Leave us alone. [*They all walk out.*]

DETECTIVES' OFFICE IN THE BLADY AGENCY.
INTERIOR. DAY.

Catherine and another operative walk into the office while Paul is shutting the door to Blady's office. Henri has remained at his desk and we hear him speaking on the phone.

HENRI (*off*): . . . the director of Compiègne College. Oh, it is? How do you do, madame . . .

Catherine leans over to take the earphone and listen in.

HENRI: . . . I am sorry to bother you . . . [*Putting his hand over the receiver, he whispers to Catherine.*] I am the director of Compiègne College [*he talks into the phone again*] . . . As I said, I don't want to bother you . . .

Catherine puts the earphone down and goes over to the little room leading to the rest rooms. She takes a dark wig from a shelf and tries it on in front of the mirror.

HENRI: I wonder if I might have a little information . . . euh . . . on one of your teachers . . . Mademoiselle Solange Dupuis.

Paul has walked into the other room; he puts his hand over Catherine's eyes.

HENRI: That's right, I want some information . . . nothing very important . . .

In the background Catherine pulls away from Paul.

PAUL: Have you thought it over?
CATHERINE: Leave me alone! I won't change my mind. When I say no, I mean no!
HENRI (off): . . . just a little information . . . how shall I put it? . . . on her morals. I want to know what sort of life she leads outside of school . . . What I'd like to find out, for instance . . .

As Henri is talking, Paul, rebuffed by Catherine, comes back into the office, while Ida goes over to Catherine, who is still adjusting her wig. Ida helps her.

CATHERINE: This is a new one. I'm on a new case. Here, give me a hand . . . yes . . . like that.

Blady is heard shouting in the background.

BLADY (off): So, I hire detectives . . . And what am I supposed to tell Monsieur Tabard? That he's paid two thousand francs to be a cuckold?
HENRI (still on the phone, and off): . . . if from time to time . . . a gentleman . . . I told you, this is strictly confidential . . .
IDA: Is it real hair?
CATHERINE: Yes, it's real.
IDA: Where did you get it?
CATHERINE: I don't know. They bought it somewhere around here. I don't know where. It's not bad, huh?
HENRI (off, still on the phone): Yes, I see, uh huh . . .

We hear the loud sound of something falling. Catherine runs out and stares at Henri's desk, now empty, in surprise.

CATHERINE: What's going on here?

We pan down to Henri lying on the floor. He has died of a heart attack; his chair has fallen down next to him and the receiver is hanging from the desk, swinging back and forth. Ida, leaning down, is trying to open Henri's collar.

CATHERINE: Oh . . . Monsieur Henri . . . Ida . . . I'd better get Monsieur Blady!

As she crosses the hall we hear Blady shouting at Antoine.

BLADY (off): . . . now I'll have to hire detectives to watch my own detectives . . . is that it?
CATHERINE (off): Monsieur Blady, come quickly . . . Monsieur Henri . . . it's awful!

Antoine runs over and leans over Henri. Blady does the same, putting his hand over Henri's heart. Paul and the bookkeeper run in. Henri lies stiffly, surrounded by his colleagues. Ida too is bent over him. The only noise is from the telephone receiver, which is swinging back and forth under the desk.

TELEPHONE (off): Hello . . . hello . . . hello!

Blady stands up, takes the receiver and speaks into the phone.

BLADY: Hello! You might as well hang up, Madame. Monsieur Henri is dead.

CEMETERY. EXTERIOR. DAY.
Ida is walking toward the camera; so are Paul, Blady, and Catherine, who is wearing a black coat. She closes her umbrella. Another detective is behind them. They are all walking along one of the cemetery rows. The last one in the procession is Antoine, who now detaches himself slowly, walking straight ahead, while

the rest of them head in a different direction. Outside the cemetery we see him walking by himself. He passes two prostitutes; one of them goes up to him. He gets off the sidewalk without responding to her, and just as he is about to cross the street, he changes his mind and goes back to the second prostitute. As they go off together he draws up his coat collar, as if to ward off a chill.

A HOTEL ROOM. INTERIOR. DAY.

A room on the ground floor. Through an opaque window we can make out a similar hotel across the street, from which a couple is emerging. Antoine removes his coat; the girl puts hers inside the closet. As he begins to remove his jacket, Antoine hands her three bills, which she puts into her purse.

THE GIRL: Look, for a little more money, I'll take all my clothes off.

Antoine takes the rest of his money out of his pocket and hands it to her.

ANTOINE: All right, here you are . . . but I'd just as soon you kept your clothes on.
THE GIRL: Thanks. If you'd like, we can stay a bit longer.
ANTOINE: No, I don't want to stay long.
THE GIRL: Okay.

STREET. EXTERIOR. DAY.

We see Lucien Darbon at the wheel of his car. The door of the Darbon house is opened. Christine, carrying her violin case in her hand, walks in.

INSIDE DARBON'S CAR. DAY.

He is driving toward a square. Through the windshield we see a small truck heading toward him. Darbon tries to avoid it. A quick cut of the two cars colliding. On the truck, a large sign: "S.O.S.– EMERGENCY REPAIRS SERVICE."

DARBON: What do you think you're doing, you idiot!

Antoine emerges from the truck looking dazed. Darbon, who hasn't recognized him, shouts.

DARBON: Your brake! Your brake!

Antoine goes back to pull the brake while Darbon gets out of his car to look over the damage. Antoine moves over to him. On his overalls we read: "HELLO S.O.S. 99–99."

DARBON (recognizing Antoine): Oh, it's you Antoine! Well, hello.
ANTOINE: Hello!

They shake hands. Antoine seems ill at ease, not only because of the accident, but probably because he has dropped the Darbon family for some time.

DARBON (cordially): What are you doing? We've all been wondering what you were up to.
ANTOINE (pointing to the inscription on his overalls): Well, I work for S.O.S. I'm a television repairman.
DARBON: That's fine.

There is heavy traffic in the background. A bus passes the two men and two drivers shout at them because they are blocking the street. A cop walks up to them.

THE COP: What's going on here? Let me have your papers, please . . .
DARBON: No, no, I'm the one to blame.

THE COP: You're taking the responsibility for this?
DARBON: Yes, I'm responsible. It's all my fault. [*The cop moves off.*] Thank you.

Antoine leans over Darbon's dented fender.

DARBON: I would have preferred to meet you under different circumstances . . . but never mind . . . it's not very serious.

THE DARBON HOME. INTERIOR. DAY.

Christine is sitting at the table in the dining room and leafing through a musical score. Behind her the television set is turned on: the commentary is very faint and on the screen are some street scenes. After a while Christine gets up, goes into the living room and throws her book on an armchair. At the sound of footsteps on the stairs she goes into the foyer, where her mother and Darbon are on their way out. He is carrying a suitcase. Mme. Darbon kisses her daughter.

MME. DARBON: Christine, we're going . . . good-bye, darling.
CHRISTINE: Good-bye, Mamma. Have a nice weekend.

The three of them move over to the door.

DARBON: Are you sure you don't want to come along? It would do you some good!
CHRISTINE: No, I can't . . . I've got to study.
DARBON: Oh, you're so serious!
MME. DARBON: Anyway, if you feel lonely, you can call Lucienne. Good-bye, darling.
CHRISTINE: All right, but I won't be bored . . . there's always TV . . . Good-bye.

Darbon kisses Christine on both cheeks.

DARBON: Well, to stay cooped up here the whole weekend . . .
But if that's what you want . . .
CHRISTINE: Good-bye.
M. AND MME. DARBON (off): Good-bye.
CHRISTINE: Good-bye.

Christine smiles to herself and goes over to the phone, next
to the television set. She dials a number.

CHRISTINE: Hello . . . S.O.S. 99–99? Can you send someone over
to 44 Avenue Edouard Vaillant, please. The television is on the
blink. Thank you.

Christine moves over behind the television set, lifts the protective screen off and begins to manipulate the inner tubes. We see
lines form on the screen, which blurs and eventually goes dark.
Christine leans over to check it, and holding the main tube in her
hands, she smiles to herself.

STREET. EXTERIOR. EVENING.

The S.O.S. truck rolls up and stops. Antoine emerges and
walks over to the rear to take out his tool kit. He goes over to the
gate of the Darbon home, pushes it open, walks in and slams it
behind him. Now the strange man in the trench coat (the one who
follows Christine) comes into view. He tries to peer inside the
garden and remains there, stationed behind the gate.

THE DARBON HOME. INTERIOR. EVENING.

Antoine, looking distant and businesslike, walks into the
living room, carrying his tool kit and a meter, which he puts on the
table. After looking over the television set, he goes behind it,
takes the plug out and examines it. Christine observes him.

ANTOINE: Oh, I see it's a Siren Voice!

He pushes the screen aside and checks the inside of the set. Christine, seemingly amused, picks up the meter Antoine has put on the table.

ANTOINE: What's going on here? Someone already took this thing off!

CHRISTINE (*examining the meter*): What a funny contraption! It's like a taxicab meter.

Antoine turns around in irritation and takes it from her hands.

ANTOINE: Look, leave that alone and let me work.

He takes the meter back to the table and begins to check out the television set with it.

Several hours later, it is night. We see the floor, with the television plug. Following the electric wire, nearby is the television screen on the floor and scattered around it are the microphone, various inner tubes and finally Antoine's tool kit marked S.O.S. The camera moves up toward the table to reveal Antoine's meter ticking away. Next, there is a close-up of the stairs, which the camera goes up. The noise of the ticking is gradually replaced by the sound of music. On the upper landing we advance toward the open door of Christine's room. In the darkness we can make out that the room is empty and the bed is made. Like a cat in the night, the camera now stalks along the hallway to the door across the way, which opens on the bedroom of M. and Mme. Darbon. On the floor inside, one slipper . . . then a second. Finally, the camera moves upward toward the bed to reveal Antoine and Christine asleep in each other's arms.

KITCHEN. INTERIOR. DAY.

Antoine and Christine are having their breakfast. Christine pours some coffee into Antoine's bowl as he looks at her.

CHRISTINE: Enough?
ANTOINE: Thanks very much.

Christine fills her own bowl. Antoine takes some dry toast, which breaks when he tries to butter it.

CHRISTINE (laughing): Oh, no, that's not the way to do it.

He smiles and puts sugar in his coffee while Christine picks up two pieces of dry toast.

CHRISTINE: I'm going to teach you something you'll never forget. How to butter dry toast without breaking it. Look, you take two pieces, you put them on top of each other, like this, then you spread the butter on . . . and thanks to the piece underneath, the one on top will never break.
ANTOINE: Hey, that's terrific.
CHRISTINE: I'll teach you everything I know . . . like how to butter toast . . . and in exchange, you'll teach me what you know. Okay?
ANTOINE: Fine.

EXTERIOR. HOUSE. DAY.

Through the half-open gate we see the strange man who always follows Christine. He's spying.

KITCHEN. INTERIOR. DAY.

Antoine is eating a buttered piece of toast.

ANTOINE: This isn't specially important . . . in a way, I guess it is
. . . but I'd rather write it down. Do you have a pencil?

Christine puts a small note pad and pencil in front of Antoine.
He writes down a few words, tears the sheet off and hands it to
Christine. She writes something on the piece of paper and hands
it back to him. They exchange several notes in this way. While
she's writing one of them, he takes a bottle opener out of the table
drawer. Reaching over for Christine's hand, he puts the circular part
of the opener around her ring finger. He stares for a while at the
makeshift wedding ring, then looks up to smile at Christine.

AN ALLEY IN A PARK. EXTERIOR. DAY.

A master shot of a wide avenue lined with trees and lawns. Antoine and Christine are coming in our direction. He raises his hand to caress her hair; they move over to a bench and sit down side by side. They look at each other. Antoine raises his hands to caress Christine's eyebrows. There is a pause. Antoine sniffles and goes through his pockets.

ANTOINE: Hell . . . I forgot my handkerchief. Do you mind lending me yours?
CHRISTINE: I have only Kleenex. Do you want one?
ANTOINE: No, I never blow my nose in paper.

She smiles at him, turns her head and looks a little worried as she sees her strange follower heading straight for their bench.

CHRISTINE: (to Antoine): Don't look now . . . that strange man is here. I think he's been following me for days. I don't know him.

Antoine steals a glance, then looks down, embarrassed.

ANTOINE: I wonder who he is?
CHRISTINE: I have no idea . . . Oh, oh . . . here he comes.

The man comes up and stops in front of the bench. Completely ignoring Antoine, he begins to speak to Christine.

THE MAN: Mademoiselle, I know that you're aware of me. [*Christine looks at Antoine.*] For a long time I watched you secretly. But for the past few days I stopped hiding, and now I know that the moment has come. You see, before discovering you, I'd never loved anybody. But between us, things will be different. We shall be the example. We shall never leave each other . . . not even for an hour. I don't work and have no responsibilities in life. You will be my sole preoccupation. I understand that this is too sudden for you to say yes at once . . . that you would first have to break off your provisional attachments to provisional people. For I am definitive. [*The man steps back, and still staring at Christine, pauses.*] I am very happy.

He turns around and moves off as the camera goes behind the backs of the young people, who are staring at him.

CHRISTINE (*turning to Antoine*): That guy is completely nuts!

Antoine is visibly disturbed as he gets to his feet.

ANTOINE: I suppose he is.

She gets up and both walk off in the opposite direction from that of the strange man. We now hear the Charles Trenet song that started the picture. Antoine, before taking Christine's arm, turns around to steal a brief glance at the man, who is far off. To the sound of Charles Trenet's song, we see them going off in the tree-lined alley.

> *The wind in one's hair*
> *Stolen kisses*
> *And shifting dreams*
> *Can anyone say*
> *Where they have gone?*
> *A little village*
> *An old belfry*
> *A lovely view*
> *Hidden away*
> *And in a cloud*
> *The beloved image*
> *Of my past*

BED AND BOARD

(Domicile Conjugal)

BED AND BOARD

(Domicile Conjugal)

CAST AND CREDITS

ANTOINE DOINEL	Jean-Pierre Léaud
CHRISTINE DOINEL	Claude Jade
MONSIEUR DARBON	Daniel Ceccaldi
MADAME DARBON	Claire Duhamel
KYOKO	Mademoiselle Hiroko
MONIQUE	Barbara Laage
CÉSARIN	Jacques Jouanneau
THE TENOR	Daniel Boulanger
THE TENOR'S WIFE	Sylvana Blasi
THE STRANGLER	Claude Vega

Screenplay, Adaptation and Dialogue by
François Truffaut, Claude de Givray, Bernard Revon
Directed by François Truffaut
Photography by Nestor Almendros
Music by Antoine Duhamel
Production
Les Films du Carrosse, Valoria Films (Paris)
and Fida Cinematografica (Rome)

OUTLINE

Outline of the screenplay based on two or three working sessions between François Truffaut, Claude de Givray and Bernard Revon.

[1]   The young couple's apartment. "Not mademoiselle—madame!"

[2]   Antoine dyes his flowers in the courtyard. One of them always retains its original color.

[3]   Christine practices her violin. Importance of the violin case.

[4]   Christine's parents. We go back to their villa. Stolen kisses.

[5]   Antoine and Christine are expecting the installation of a telephone.

[6]   We meet Monsieur X, the strangler.

[7]   The importance of the café where they make their phone calls.

[8]   Antoine runs into one of his former fellow workers from S.O.S.

[9]   First meeting with the moocher.

[10]   The waitress who is in love with Antoine.

[11]   The tenor and his Italian wife. He throws her fur coat down the stairs.

[12]   Antoine makes his living by dyeing flowers; in a moment of absent-mindedness he botches the job. He gives it up.

[13]   The young couple has dinner at the café. They eat on credit.

[14]   They are advised they are about to get their phone.

[15]   Christine is too embarrassed to remind her pupils' parents to pay for their lessons. We have to find a gimmick so that Antoine gets the money from them.

[16]   Second meeting with Monsieur X, the strangler.

[17]   Antoine notices that Christine's breasts are not of the same size.

[18]   They have to thank the Senator for getting them their phone.

[19]   Antoine accompanies Christine to a building that has a doctor's name plate on the front door, with the notation "Gynecologist." He notices it but fails to understand the implications.

[20]   Second meeting with the moocher.

[21]   The American Hydraulic Plant is looking for an ambitious young employee.

[22]   Antoine is hired by mistake.

[23]   A development in the life of the young couple: Christine is pregnant.

[24] Life inside the office: The American boss, the wise guy, Nicole, and the secretary in whom Antoine confides, etc.

[25] Life inside the apartment house: The tenor, the love-starved waitress, the Pétain follower who is a voluntary recluse, etc.

[26] Third meeting with the moocher. A boy or a girl?

[27] At the clinic: A difficult confinement. Antoine spends the evening trying to find someone to whom he can announce he's a father.

[28] The baby at home; the in-laws. An argument over the baby's name: Will it be Alphonse or Ghislain?

[29] Antoine announces that he's writing a novel.

[30] Fourth meeting with the moocher.

[31] One evening there's nothing to eat; Antoine and Christine will dine on their son's baby food.

[32] They see their neighbor "the strangler" do a take-off on Delphine Seyrig on TV. It turns out that he's a professional entertainer.

[33] They knock down a wall in the apartment to make a room for the baby.

[34] A Japanese family visits the Hydraulic Plant.

[35] Beginning of the affair with the Japanese girl.

[36] Christine wears eyeglasses; Antoine rather likes them on her.

[37]   Christine finds out all about the Japanese girl through a love message concealed in a bouquet of flowers. There is a scene.

[38]   The household is divided; Antoine now sleeps on a mattress in the dining room.

[39]   The couple breaks up.

[40]   Antoine is getting fed up with his Japanese sweetheart. From the restaurant where they're having dinner together, he calls Christine three times and makes up with her.

[41]   Antoine goes back to his wife.

[42]   The gag about the singer. End.

WORK NOTES

*These notes from François Truffaut to Claude de Givray and
Bernard Revon were the basis for the first draft of the scenario.*

ACT I—THEY ARE MARRIED.
[1] To avoid the traditional exposition, which is generally documentary and anti-dramatic, we should try to find some amusing way
to convey to the public:
    a. that Antoine is married;
    b. that his métier is to dye flowers.

[2] Christine gives violin lessons either in her own home or at the
homes of her pupils. This is not a matter of choosing between the
two, but simply means that we can take advantage of both situations.

We should come up with two or three gags around the violin
case. At some point Christine might use the case as a piece of
luggage, packing her things into it and saying: "I'm going home to
Mother." Or else, assuming that Christine is assembling a layette
without Antoine's knowledge, she can hide the baby things in the
violin case.

[3] Somewhere in this first act we will have to re-introduce Antoine's in-laws (Daniel Ceccaldi and Claire Duhamel) and probably
go back to their villa on the outskirts of Paris in order to recall
Stolen Kisses. This time, it is Christine who will steal a kiss in the
wine cellar.

[4]   It is also in this first act that we should situate the apartment house where the young couple lives, as well as several of the main characters:

   a. Monsieur X (the strangler).

   b. The love-starved waitress who constantly hounds Antoine. It's as if she were the aggressive male and he a timid young maiden.

   c. The moocher on the street.

   d. The parking agent.

   e. The voluntary recluse.

   f. The opera singer.

[5]   We must establish the important role that the café on the ground floor of the building plays in all their lives (prior to the dinner invitation at their in-laws).

NOTES ON THE FIRST ACT

We might start the picture with the opera singer. A man is impatiently pacing back and forth on the landing; the door to his apartment is half-open. After circling around several times, he suddenly throws a fur coat, a purse and a hat down the stairway. His wife comes out on the landing. Still buttoning her dress and protesting mildly at her husband's impatience, she follows him down the stairs. The explanation to this scene is provided, a few minutes later, by the voluntary recluse, who is permanently stationed at his window: the man is an opera singer and his wife is chronically late.

In connection with the flowers that Antoine dyes, let us bear in mind that while the reds turn yellow, or the yellows turn red, one of the flowers, for some reason unknown even to Antoine, always retains its original color.

The young couple does not have a telephone. We must introduce this idea somewhere at the very beginning, since it explains the importance of the café in their lives. The problem of the phone will crop up again in the first scene with the in-laws.

One of the problems of this first act is that it features a whole series of oddball characters (Monsieur X—the strangler, the moocher, the love-starved waitress and the opera singer) who might put one another at a disadvantage. One way to handle that might be to make some of them less caricatural.

ACT II—*She's expecting.*
[1] Antoine dyes his flowers in a courtyard. One day, when his attention is distracted by something taking place on the other side of the yard (perhaps in a maid's room on the ground floor), he ruins his dyeing job and is fired.

A footnote: If Antoine was to work in the courtyard of the building in which he lives with Christine, it would give us the advantage of linking all of the elements together.

[2] The first scene in the café is the telephone call to the in-laws; the second would show that the young couple often eats there— probably on credit.

[3] They finally succeed in getting their telephone,* thanks to Antoine's father-in-law, or rather through a customer of his at the garage, who happens to be a Senator.

[4] At one point the young couple contemplates pawning Christine's violin case, which would give us another variation on the empty violin case.

[5] Monsieur X, who is suspected of being a strangler, will again appear in this Act.

---

* In France the telephone is a state monopoly. A very long waiting period is required to have one installed, except for the lucky few who happen to have official connections.

[6]   We have to come up with ideas to show that the young couple has money problems.

[7]   The in-laws manage to get them a telephone and also offer them a TV set. Antoine writes an insolent thank-you note to the Senator who's pulled strings for them, which leads to a heated argument between the young couple. They will also try to sell their TV set.

[8]   Christine discovers that she is pregnant—and so does the public—before Antoine is aware of it. (Unless something better comes along, we might use the gimmick of the doctor's name plate in front of the building.)

[9]   The moocher on the street hits Antoine up for the second time.

ACT III—*He works for the Americans.*
[1]   Antoine is hired by the Hydraulic Plant as the result of a misunderstanding. We introduce an American boss and a few members of the staff: the wise guy (Pierre Fabre), a young secretary named Nicole and an older, rather attractive secretary in whom he confides.

[2]   We should come up with some ideas that might illustrate Christine's pregnancy. We might be able to do something with records on natural childbirth.

[3]   Life inside the apartment house, via the tenor, the love-starved waitress and the voluntary recluse.

[4]   Life inside the café. Here is where we see the influence of

television one morning when all the customers, in giving their orders to the barman, repeat a sentence used in a television commercial the evening before.

[5]   The third meeting with the moocher.

[6]   The day of Christine's confinement. The Clinic. Antoine runs around looking for people to whom he can announce that he is a father.

ACT IV—*The baby.*
[1]   The baby at the home of Antoine's in-laws.

[2]   At the Hydraulic Plant the young secretary takes up a collection for a present for Antoine's baby. The wise guy refuses to chip in. He tells the story of a chiseler who, on each new job, after announcing his mother had just died, would pick up the proceeds of the office collection and walk off the job.

[3]   Antoine's fourth meeting with the moocher. (We should make sure that these meetings do not follow immediately upon scenes illustrating the young couple's money difficulties; the public might be irritated by the contradiction.)

[4]   For want of foresight one day, Antoine and Christine, having nothing to eat, fall back on the baby food.

[5]   Upon seeing Monsieur X, the strangler, on a television program one evening, they discover that he is a professional entertainer who does imitations of Delphine Seyrig. Christine is quite amused, but Antoine appears to be distressed.

ACT V—*Trouble in the Doinel ménage.*

[1] Some Japanese clients visit the Hydraulic Plant. While demonstrating his model boats, Antoine can hardly keep his eyes off lovely Kyoko. When she has to go to the ladies' room, Antoine will show her the way.

[2] Beginning of the love story with the Japanese girl. She shares a flat with a roommate; Antoine can't understand a word of what they say to each other.

[3] Christine finds out about the affair and lets Antoine know that she knows by staging a little Oriental *mise en scène*: he comes home one evening to find his wife all dolled up in a Japanese costume.

[4] Crisis in the household: Antoine will sleep on a mattress in the dining room.

[5] When the in-laws invite themselves over for dinner, the young couple has to put up a good front and push all the furniture back in place.

[6] That night, they break up. (We might be able to make use of the violin case in this scene.) Antoine is the one who leaves home. After he's slammed the door behind him, Christine stands there, munching a piece of chocolate, with tears in her eyes.

[7] The separation. Antoine lives in a small hotel on the Place Clichy. From time to time he comes home to see the baby, Alphonse.

[8] The scene in the restaurant with the Japanese girl. Antoine will interrupt their tête-à-tête three times by stepping out to call up Christine and tell her how bored he is with the Japanese girl.

[9]   Antoine goes back to Christine. We loop the circle by having Antoine imitate the behavior of the enraged opera singer at the beginning of the film, throwing Christine's coat down the stairs. The tenor's Italian wife says: "You see, darling, now they are truly in love!" as he responds with a skeptical look.

FINAL SCREENPLAY

STREET. EXTERIOR. DAY.

Christine is walking along the sidewalk, carrying her violin case. She stops at a fruit stand.

CHRISTINE: (off): Two pounds of tangerines, please.
FRUIT VENDOR (off): There you are, mademoiselle.
CHRISTINE (off): No, not mademoiselle—madame!

Christine's next stop is at a newsstand.

CHRISTINE: This magazine, please.
NEWS DEALER: Here you are.
CHRISTINE: Look . . . that poster of Nureyev . . . May I have it?
NEWS DEALER: Sure!
CHRISTINE: Thank you very much.
NEWS DEALER: Help yourself.
CHRISTINE: Lovely—really great! How much?
NEWS DEALER: Two francs.
CHRISTINE: Thank you, monsieur.
NEWS DEALER: Thank you, mademoiselle.
CHRISTINE: No, not mademoiselle—madame!

STAIRWAY OF THE DOINEL APARTMENT HOUSE.
INTERIOR. DAY.

Christine starts up the stairs behind an old man who's wearing the uniform of a parking agent. He stands against the wall to let her pass.

PARKING AGENT: You go ahead, I'm slow.

He stares at her legs as she moves up and out of sight. Christine reaches her landing. We hear a tenor voice doing vocal exercises. The door to her apartment is open; just as she's about to go in, Antoine rushes out.

ANTOINE: Hello.

CHRISTINE: Hello.

They exchange a brief kiss.

ANTOINE: Excuse me, I'm late. I forgot the red!

Hurrying down the stairs, Antoine runs into the parking agent, still going up.

ANTOINE: Hi there!

COURTYARD OF THE DOINEL BUILDING.
EXTERIOR. DAY.

Antoine goes over to a little wooden shed that he uses as a workshop. Through the open door we see paraphernalia of a florist's shop. In the courtyard, lined up against the shed, are several huge bunches of carnations of different colors.

Antoine goes inside to pick up a can of red spray, then goes over to a plastic pail containing a big bunch of white carnations. Ginette, the café waitress, comes up to him.

GINETTE: Hello, Antoine, how is it going? So you're dyeing them red? That's an old trick; we used to do it in school. When I was a kid, we'd stick a flower in the inkwell; it would turn black, or blue. Then we'd stick it in our notebooks. It was so messy, we'd get hell!

ANTOINE (off): Look, they're already pink.

A man is looking down at them from a window on the first floor. He is an elderly man who has become a voluntary recluse since the death of Marshal Pétain.

THE RECLUSE: They're going to ban those products. They said so on television.
ANTOINE: What the hell for?
THE RECLUSE: Because of water pollution. They're even going to ban shaving cream. From now on everyone's going to have to use electric razors!

All of the carnations are now bright red with the exception of one, which has remained white.

ANTOINE: Look how red they are.
GINETTE: That was quick! My hands are still red.
ANTOINE: That's because of the immersion heater . . .
GINETTE: Isn't that funny! One of them is still white.
ANTOINE: Yes, it's strange. That always happens and I can't figure out why it is.

Césarin, the café owner who is Ginette's boss, emerges from the wine cellar.

CÉSARIN: Hi, Antoine, how's the art work? Damn it, Ginette, what are you doing there? I pay you good money and you just goof around there!

As Césarin goes into the café, Ginette moves over to Antoine and speaks to him in a confidential manner.

GINETTE: Know what I did? I bought new pajamas, threw the pants

away and kept only the top. What do you think about that?
ANTOINE (*nonplussed*): Not a thing!

Ginette goes over to the other side of the yard where little Christophe is playing with a balloon. A funny-looking man, a tenant of the house, walks in.

THE TENANT (*to Ginette*): How do you do? [*To Antoine.*] Hello. I see the flowers got here. The blues are red now.
THE RECLUSE (*leaning out of the window*): No, it's the other way around: the red ones are blue!

Césarin, at the rear window of the café which overlooks the courtyard, is talking to one of his customers, a Sanitation Department employee who works in the sewer system.

CÉSARIN: Well, her mother's dead. That's an old story. At the time, I said to her: "Listen, Madame Fournier, just behave yourself! My little radio isn't bothering anybody, so stop making trouble for me" and that's when she says: "So, sue me!" I'm sorry, but I pay taxes on my radio set and what does she do? She makes buttonholes, that's what! How do you like that? I should have reported her right then and there, but it's been going on for ten years so what can I do about it now? I'd look like an idiot, you know what I mean . . .

The customer loses interest in Césarin's monologue; he gets up and walks out into the courtyard, while Césarin rambles on.

CÉSARIN (*off*): If I had to do it over again, I'd report her!
THE CUSTOMER: I'll be back.
CÉSARIN (*off*): Right. But I am going to report her!

Christophe talks to the customer.

CHRISTOPHE: Look—they turned red!

The customer walks over to Antoine.

THE CUSTOMER: Say, I was looking at you work. Why don't you go into business for yourself? [*The café telephone rings.*] I once knew a florist, an English lady . . .
CÉSARIN (off): Hey, Antoine! Telephone!
ANTOINE: For me?
CÉSARIN: Yes. Hurry up!

Antoine runs over to the café, climbs in the open window and goes over to the telephone on the counter. Césarin, in the background, is monologuing with another customer.

CÉSARIN: What's right is right, after all. I don't mind paying my taxes, but . . .
ANTOINE: Hello . . . Oh, hello, Mother . . . I'm fine. All right, I'll call her . . . just hold on . . . [*Antoine runs out into the yard and raises his head toward his apartment.*] Christine! Christine! [*His wife doesn't respond, but he spots a neighbor at another window.*] Could you call my wife, please . . . tell her her mother's on the phone?
THE NEIGHBOR: Sure.

CAFÉ. INTERIOR. DAY.
Christine, crossing the courtyard, comes into the café and picks up the receiver.

CHRISTINE: Hello, Mamma . . . I can't hear.

Ginette, on her way out to the courtyard, passes Christine.

GINETTE: Those garbage cans . . .

In the courtyard Ginette and the concierge get into a heated argument over the garbage pails. The two women shriek at each other throughout Christine's phone conversation.

GINETTE: Can't you stop that with the garbage pails . . .
CHRISTINE: Hello, hello. Yes . . . I don't think Antoine has anything planned. Can we bring anything?

The altercation in the courtyard is increasingly violent. The two women are fighting over the garbage pails, with one pulling them toward the right and the other toward the left.

CHRISTINE: I said . . . do you want us to bring you anything? All right. No later than eight-thirty. That's right. See you tonight!

In the courtyard, the concierge is now grumbling to herself.

THE CONCIERGE: If the new management refuses to pay for new garbage cans, I'll go right on using these old ones.

Crossing the courtyard, Christine stops to talk to Antoine.

CHRISTINE: We're invited to dinner at eight tonight. Okay?
ANTOINE: Okay. I'll be up as soon as I finish this.
CHRISTINE: Right.

As she goes into the building, she exchanges a greeting with Ginette, who is coming out into the courtyard. Ginette goes over to Antoine.

GINETTE: I want you and I'll get you!

Antoine, a little taken aback, turns to the little boy.

ANTOINE: Here, Christophe, give me a hand. Carry this over there.

DOINEL LANDING. INTERIOR. DAY.

On the floor of the Doinel apartment, their next-door neighbor (a tenor) is pacing back and forth; he seems very agitated. Christine looks at him, then goes into her apartment. The man impatiently checks the time on his watch.

WOMAN (off; *she speaks with a strong Italian accent*): Coming, dear! Here I am, I'm almost ready. I'll be right there.

The apartment next door to the Doinels' is open. The man steps inside, emerging a few moments later with a fur coat and a purse, which he throws down the staircase. His wife appears at the door. She turns the lights off, locks the door and hastily finishes buttoning her blouse as she follows her husband down the stairs.

THE TENOR'S WIFE: *O Dio mio! Che vita! Ma che vita da cane! O Dio mio!*

COURTYARD. EXTERIOR. LATE AFTERNOON.

Antoine, closing shop, looks up as the agitated man comes out of the building, followed by his wife, who stops to put on her fur coat and then hurries to catch up with her husband.

THE RECLUSE: You can set your watch by him: it's seven-fifteen. That guy is just like clockwork! He's a tenor at the Opéra. You know them, Antoine . . . they live on your floor.
ANTOINE: Yes, they're our neighbors.
THE RECLUSE: That's it. He's always right on time. That's why he's always mad at his wife, because she's like you with your flowers: a little red here, a little blue there . . .

Looking toward the street, the recluse suddenly interrupts what he was saying and whispers down to Antoine.

THE RECLUSE: Antoine, look over there!

The young man who is coming into the courtyard looks straight ahead and without a word goes into the building. As he goes inside, Antoine stares after him thoughtfully.

THE DARBON VILLA. EXTERIOR. EVENING.
The lights go on as we overhear a voice inside.

MADAME DARBON (off): Christine, we need a bottle of wine. Would you go down to the cellar to get it?

THE DARBON VILLA. INTERIOR. EVENING.
Christine opens the door to the cellar while Antoine and Darbon are talking in the next room.

DARBON: The funniest thing is that you had to hold the personnel back . . . they wanted to work!
CHRISTINE: Antoine, can you give me a hand?
DARBON: Yes, that's right . . . go ahead.

Antoine follows Christine to the cellar. She points to a bottle on the stacks.

CHRISTINE: That bottle, please.

Antoine takes it and is about to go back upstairs when Christine holds him back.

CHRISTINE: Wait a minute.

Gently pushing him against the wall, she kisses him. They exchange a reminiscent smile before walking upstairs together.

DARBON (off): He had a Mercedes, so his political friends said: "Look, a foreign car makes a bad impression." So he got a Citroën and I took the Mercedes off his hands. I won't have any trouble selling it . . .

Darbon is already seated at the dining-room table and his wife is beginning to serve as Antoine and Christine sit down. Antoine notices some exotic-looking flowers on the television set.

ANTOINE: I see you have striglias.

DARBON: What?

ANTOINE: Striglias.

DARBON: Is that what they are?

ANTOINE: Yes . . . many people mistake them for oubliglias.

MME. DARBON: Is that so?

DARBON: I see.

MME. DARBON: My neighbor gave them to me because I helped her paint her attic. Let me have your plates.

DARBON: Oh, I thought you brought them . . . for Mother's Day . . . last week.

CHRISTINE: Oh, was it Mother's Day? I'm so sorry, Mamma, I forgot all about it. I'm really sorry . . .

ANTOINE: Anyway, Mother's Day is a Nazi invention.

DARBON: Is that so?

MME. DARBON: Really?

ANTOINE: Yes . . . during the war . . . the Germans . . .

MME. DARBON (*interrupting*): They stand up very well, don't they? This morning I put an aspirin in the water.

ANTOINE: Aspirin in the water?

MME. DARBON: Yes.

ANTOINE: That's real nonsense. What you've got to do is to cut the stem.

MME. DARBON: I do that too . . . every morning. I cut the stems about half an inch . . .

ANTOINE (*laughing*): You cut the stems half an inch and put them back in the water?

MME. DARBON: Yes . . .

ANTOINE: That's useless too. What you've got to do is to cut them in the water so that no air gets in and the water travels straight up the stem into the flower.

DARBON: Did your Japanese expert tell you that?

ANTOINE: Yes.

MME. DARBON: The Japanese know all about flowers. With them, it's an art.

ANTOINE (pompously): It's floral art! [Notices that his plate is empty.] What about me? Don't I get any soup?

MME. DARBON (filling his plate): I'm sorry.

DARBON: By the way, I spoke to the Senator . . . he is quite interested in your idea for a self-service flower stand. He might invest in it.

ANTOINE: Well, I'm not interested anymore. I've thought it over and . . .

DARBON: I see . . .

CHRISTINE: There's too much spoilage. Isn't that right, Antoine?

ANTOINE: Yes.

CHRISTINE: It might work near a cemetery because they could make wreaths with the flowers that are left over.

ANTOINE: The point is I'm working on a much more interesting project. I'm studying a process that will enable me to turn the flowers Absolute Red.

DARBON: I see. Well, I'll tell the Senator to forget about the self-service. In any case, he's promised me that you'll get your telephone within the next three weeks.

CHRISTINE: Great! The pupils will be able to call me directly.

MME. DARBON: By the way, did you get the message about little Marianne?

CHRISTINE: Yes. Her dentist canceled the appointment and she came by.

DARBON: Is that the little virtuoso who plays better than you do?

CHRISTINE: Don't exaggerate! She's very gifted. The only trouble is that her mother always forgets to pay for the lesson and I don't know how to remind her . . .

ANTOINE: Well, leave it to me. I'll ask her!

CHRISTINE: But you're down there in the courtyard . . .

ANTOINE: Never mind. When she comes down I'll grab her and I'll ask her.

DARBON: Children, I've got an idea . . . a great idea. Listen . . . [He pauses.] . . . When the mother forgets to pay, you just let her walk out.

CHRISTINE: Just like that?

DARBON: You do nothing. Just close the door and then play a tune so that Antoine will know. That way he knows whether he should tackle the woman.

CHRISTINE: Swell!

MME. DARBON: That's a good idea.

ANTOINE: Not bad, not bad . . .

DARBON: You bet, it's not bad . . .

CHRISTINE: What shall I play?
DARBON: Wait a minute.

He puts his hands up to his face in order to concentrate, while Antoine starts humming a melody.

MME. DARBON: "The Bridge on the River Kwai."
DARBON: No, not that . . . She'd know there's something funny.

He begins to hum a folk song.

MME. DARBON: No.
DARBON: You're right . . . we need something livelier . . . Wait a minute . . .
MME. DARBON: "Autumn Leaves"?
DARBON: Too slow!
CHRISTINE: "Carmen" . . . or "The Jewel Song"?
DARBON: What's that?
MME. DARBON: It's no good. Nobody knows it.
DARBON: Let's keep trying.
CHRISTINE: What about "La Marseillaise"?
DARBON: Of course!
MME. DARBON: Why "La Marseillaise"?
DARBON: Because it's a classic. Nobody will notice it. It's just right . . . No, no, children . . . we can't use that.
CHRISTINE: Why not?
DARBON: You can't play "La Marseillaise."
ANTOINE: Why not?
DARBON (dramatically): Because you can't fiddle around with the national anthem! [They all burst into laughter.] That's culture, that's culture!

THE DARBON VILLA. EXTERIOR. NIGHT.
A master shot of the Darbon villa with all the lights on. We

overhear the sounds of the cheerful conversation that is taking place inside.

DOINEL STAIRCASE. INTERIOR. EVENING.

Antoine and Christine are going upstairs when the lights go out.

CHRISTINE: I'll get the light. [*As she fumbles for the light switch, a hand grabs hers in the dark.*] Oh!

As the lights go on, she is startled all over again for the strange man is in front of her. Without a word he steps aside and continues to walk down the stairs. Christine whispers to Antoine.

CHRISTINE: There's something creepy about that guy!
ANTOINE: Did you ask Madame Martin who he is . . . where he comes from?
CHRISTINE: She doesn't know. He's a sublet. He's been living here for three months. He hasn't had a single visitor, or even a letter, in all that time.

Antoine, behind Christine, turns sinister.

ANTOINE: Did you notice his long hairy hands, with forked fingers and sharp nails that come out at night and . . . grab at women's legs!

Christine turns around in alarm, then, realizing Antoine is kidding her, begins to run up the stairs. He follows her, still menacing.

CHRISTINE: Cut it out!
ANTOINE: . . . to grab at women's legs . . .
CHRISTINE: Stop that!

DOINEL APARTMENT. INTERIOR. NIGHT.
    Christine is in bed, reading a book; Antoine is removing his tie.

ANTOINE: Damn! I forgot the light. [*After turning the light out in the next room, he comes back into the bedroom and begins to undress.*] Don't look!
CHRISTINE: I'm reading.
ANTOINE: I think naked men are disgusting. I mean it . . . they're ugly. If I were a woman, I couldn't stand seeing a naked man. They're repulsive!

CHRISTINE: Not all men . . .
ANTOINE: All men. All of them!
CHRISTINE: All except one!

As he hops into bed Antoine notices the Nureyev poster on the wall, over the bed.

ANTOINE: Who the hell is he?
CHRISTINE: That's Nureyev. He's a great dancer! I think he's terribly handsome. The news dealer gave it to me. [*Christine puts her book down as Antoine stretches out. She pulls at her nightgown*

and looks down.] My poor breasts; if I ever have a baby, I certainly won't be able to breast-feed it.

ANTOINE: Neither will I. He'll have to feed himself. Let's have a look . . .

CHRISTINE: Listen . . .

ANTOINE: I just want to see . . . What's wrong with them? [*He peers under her nightgown and seems concerned.*] Say, they don't match!

CHRISTINE: What are you talking about . . . you're crazy!

ANTOINE: No, I mean it . . . one of them is bigger than the other.

CHRISTINE: That's not true.

ANTOINE: It is so!

CHRISTINE: But isn't everybody like that?

ANTOINE: Not at all. We ought to give them names to tell them apart. We could call them Laurel and Hardy.

CHRISTINE: Stop it!

ANTOINE: Why not? If you want, this one can be Don Quixote and we'd call the little one Sancho Panza.

CHRISTINE: That's not funny! Let's turn the light out.

Antoine stretches in the darkness.

ANTOINE: Oh, isn't it wonderful to lie in bed at night, all warm and cozy!

BEDROOM. INTERIOR. MORNING.

Christine is almost dressed. She draws the curtains, then goes over to the bed.

CHRISTINE: Antoine, wake up. My pupil is coming. [*Buried under the bedclothes, he doesn't move. Christine sits down by his side.*] Six sheep, five sheep, four sheep, three sheep, two sheep, one sheep, zero sheep! [*Antoine leaps out of bed.*]

FOYER OF THE DOINEL APARTMENT. INTERIOR. DAY.
Antoine opens the door. A little girl and her mother walk in.

ANTOINE: Hello, Marianne.
THE MOTHER: Good morning, monsieur.
ANTOINE: I'll call my wife. She'll be here in a minute. Christine! Christine!
CHRISTINE (off): Yes?
ANTOINE: They're here for the lesson.
CHRISTINE (off): I'll be right there. [*She comes in.*]
ANTOINE: If you'll excuse me, I'll leave you now . . .
CHRISTINE: Good morning, madame.
THE MOTHER: Good morning, madame.
CHRISTINE: How are you, Marianne? [*While the mother removes the little girl's coat, Antoine, standing behind the woman, signals to his wife not to forget the money.*] Come in, please. And excuse me . . . I'm a little late this morning. Did you practice, Marianne?
MARIANNE: Yes.
CHRISTINE: Good. Your scales and your sostenutos?
MARIANNE: Yes.
CHRISTINE: Very good.
THE MOTHER: She's practiced about an hour every day.
CHRISTINE: Fine. Let's start right in with the "Little Concert."

[*She tunes the violin.*] All right. Remember your attacks and watch the tone.

We listen for a while as Marianne begins to play.

STREET. EXTERIOR. DAY.

Quick cut of an S.O.S. truck pulling up in front of the building.

COURTYARD. EXTERIOR. DAY.

Antoine is coloring his carnations. We hear the sound of Marianne's violin lesson upstairs. In the background a young man, wearing the S.O.S. uniform, enters the courtyard and knocks at the concierge's door. There is no answer. One of the tenants, passing by, greets Antoine.

THE TENANT: Good morning, Monsieur Doinel. How are things?
ANTOINE: Good morning.
S.O.S. MAN: Anybody in? Concierge! Nobody home? [*He walks over to Antoine.*] Excuse me . . . could you tell me . . . Hey, Doinel!
ANTOINE: Hi! How are you? You look the same.
S.O.S. MAN: I'm okay. How are you?
ANTOINE: Same as always.
S.O.S. MAN: Nothing new here. What're you doing?
ANTOINE: What you see: I dye flowers.
S.O.S. MAN: Your own business?
ANTOINE: No, I work for a florist shop down the block.
S.O.S. MAN: Is that so? Say, that looks like hard work. My grandfather always told me that it takes a lazy man to work hard! [*Antoine laughs.*] Are you married?
ANTOINE: Yes. We live right here. Hear that violin up there?
S.O.S. MAN: Yes.

ANTOINE: That's my wife. She's a musician; she gives lessons.

S.O.S. MAN: A musician, huh? You always did like nice little middle-class girls!

ANTOINE: I never looked at it that way. I like girls who've got nice parents. I love parents, so long as they're not mine.

S.O.S. MAN: Is that right?

The parking agent walks over to them.

PARKING AGENT: Say . . . . you . . .

S.O.S. MAN: What . . . what the hell does he want . . .

PARKING AGENT: Is that your truck in front of the house?

S.O.S. MAN: Yes. What of it?

PARKING AGENT: You can't park there.

S.O.S. MAN: Why not? It's not in anybody's way.

PARKING AGENT: I already gave you a ticket. Do you want another one?

S.O.S. MAN: Sure, Dad, make it a pair! Christ . . . I'm fed up with that crap! [He turns to Antoine.] Say, I'm supposed to fix a TV set. D'you know a Desdoigts . . .

ANTOINE: You mean Monsieur Desbois. He's right up there. [Antoine calls out.] Monsieur Desbois! That's funny . . . Monsieur Desbois!

S.O.S. MAN: Maybe he's gone out.

ANTOINE: I don't think so. He hasn't left his house for twenty-five years . . . he's a sort of voluntary recluse.

S.O.S. MAN: Is that so?

ANTOINE: He swore he wouldn't go out till Marshal Whosis . . .

S.O.S. MAN: You mean Marshal Juin?

ANTOINE: No, older than him . . . You know, the guy who ran France during the war . . .

S.O.S. MAN: Oh, Marshal Pétain!

ANTOINE: That's who: Marshal Pétain. Well, he swore he won't go out until Pétain is buried in Verdun!

S.O.S. MAN: What does he do?

ANTOINE (*calls again*): Monsieur Desbois . . .

The voluntary recluse on the first floor opens his window.

ANTOINE (*off*): It's the TV repairman!
THE VOLUNTARY RECLUSE: It's about time! Hurry up!
S.O.S. MAN: Take it easy!

As he heads for the stairs, Antoine stops him.

ANTOINE: Hey, how is Josianne?
S.O.S. MAN: What about Josianne?
ANTOINE: Did you marry her?
S.O.S. MAN: No, no. She quit work to marry—you'll never guess who—an astronaut! Those guys get big pay and they're always away! She lives on Avenue Foch, can you beat that? She's got it made. He knocked her up . . . that's why he married her. What I think is that she did it purposely . . .

The violin scales have stopped as he speaks and now we hear the opening bars of "La Marseillaise." Antoine comes to attention.

ANTOINE: Oh, excuse me. I'll be right back. So long.
S.O.S. MAN: So long.

The door of the building opens to make way for the little violin player and her mother. Antoine goes over to them.

ANTOINE (*to Marianne*): Hello. You're getting good! [*To the mother.*] She's really made great progress, hasn't she?
THE MOTHER: Thanks to Madame Doinel . . . she's a wonderful teacher.
ANTOINE: Yes . . . but when I hear the violin, I can never tell whether it's my wife or Marianne playing. [*He turns to Marianne.*]

Soon you'll be giving the lessons and my wife will be paying you. Right?
THE MOTHER: My goodness! I forgot to pay your wife!
ANTOINE: No hurry . . . some other time . . .
THE MOTHER: Yes, yes. I forgot last time too!
ANTOINE: Never mind . . . it can wait.

The woman takes some money out of her purse and hands it to Antoine.

THE MOTHER: This is for two lessons.
ANTOINE: Well, thank you. Good-bye. . . .

Rather pleased with himself, Antoine watches the woman and her daughter go out of the courtyard, then raises his head toward the windows of his apartment and whistles the final strains of "La Marseillaise."

PARIS STREET. EXTERIOR. DAY.
Weaving in and out of traffic, Antoine is carrying a heavy contraption over his shoulder. A tall, lanky fellow, resembling a scarecrow, comes up to him.

ANTOINE: Oh, hello.
THE MOOCHER: Hi, Doinel. What's that?
ANTOINE: It's a library staircase.
THE MOOCHER: Say, can you let me have thirty francs?
ANTOINE: Sure.
THE MOOCHER: All right.
ANTOINE: So long.

The two men walk off in opposite directions.

THE DOINEL APARTMENT. INTERIOR. DAY.

We hear Christine's violin and see the door open. Antoine comes in, still carrying the contraption. After closing the door, he looks up.

ANTOINE: What are you doing?

Christine, perched on a table, stops playing.

CHRISTINE: I'm practicing.

Antoine walks over to the table and caresses her legs.

ANTOINE: Why can't you practice down here?
CHRISTINE: I'm trying to get over my stage fright. I got panicky at the last concert and I realized it was on account of the orchestra pit. It wasn't really stage fright; it was looking down at the pit that made me dizzy, so I'm trying to get used to heights. [*Antoine is still caressing her legs.*] Say, what are you doing? I'm coming down.
ANTOINE: No, no, I'm thinking about something.
CHRISTINE: I'll bet you are. Let me get down.
ANTOINE: No! Close your eyes and don't move.
CHRISTINE: No, I know what you're going to do.
ANTOINE: Absolutely not. Nothing's further from my mind. Just close your eyes; I won't touch you.
CHRISTINE: Promise?
ANTOINE: Scout's honor!
CHRISTINE: You're putting me on . . . you never were a boy scout!
ANTOINE: You bet I wasn't. Okay, you're closing your eyes, right?
CHRISTINE (*with one eye open*): Yes.
ANTOINE (*going to the door*): Just keep them closed.
CHRISTINE: Yes, yes.

Antoine comes back with the library staircase, which he puts down next to the table.

ANTOINE: Now, open them.
CHRISTINE: What's that?
ANTOINE: A library staircase. I've always wanted one.
CHRISTINE (*stepping off the table*): You're crazy! We don't even have a library!
ANTOINE: We've got to begin somewhere!

Christine steps into the next room and comes back holding a long wire.

CHRISTINE: I've got a surprise for you too! [*As they talk, they follow the wire, which leads them to a brand-new telephone in the bedroom.*] Look! The Senator came through . . . We've got a beautiful phone—the latest model. What do you think?
ANTOINE: Not bad . . . [*He sits down by the phone as she goes into the next room.*] Okay, but before I thank him, I want to know if it works. I'll call to check the time. What's that number again?
CHRISTINE (*off*): Odeon 84-00.
ANTOINE: Odeon 84 . . .
CHRISTINE (*off*): 0 . . . 0.
ANTOINE: 0 . . . 0. Hello . . . Cochin Hospital? Sorry, wrong number. [*He hangs up.*] I wanted to get the time and I got a hospital!
CHRISTINE (*off*): Well then, dial the hospital, maybe you'll get the time!
ANTOINE: That's an idea!

THE DOINEL APARTMENT. INTERIOR. EVENING.
Antoine, seated at the desk, has just finished writing a letter. He puts his pen down and lights a cigarette. Christine steps out of the kitchen.

CHRISTINE: How's the letter?
ANTOINE: It's almost finished.

CHRISTINE: Can I see it? [*He gets up and she sits down at the desk to read.*] "Dear Senator: Thanks to you, it took me eight days to get what the average Frenchman spends years waiting for!" You're out of your mind! You can't send that!

ANTOINE: Why not? It's true, isn't it?

CHRISTINE: Listen . . . Lucien knocked himself out . . . the Senator is a customer of his . . . you simply can't do this!

ANTOINE: Well, I'm sorry, but that's the way I feel. If you don't like it, write him yourself!

CHRISTINE: I will! But you're a selfish monster. Everybody has to help you . . . you do nothing for anybody!

ANTOINE: I didn't ask for anything! I don't give a damn about the phone!

CHRISTINE: That's right, you don't give a damn, but when we're bored, we can get in touch with friends on that phone!

ANTOINE: When we're bored? I don't know what boredom is! I know some people get bored, but I don't know what it means. There are always things to do . . . cutting the pages of a book . . . the crossword puzzle . . . taking notes . . . there's always something one can do. I wish there were a thirty-hour day because I'm never bored. In fact, I wish I was an old man because then I could get by on five hours' sleep. Oh, what's the use of talking . . . I'm going to the toilet!

Antoine walks out of the room as Christine begins to write the letter.

COURTYARD OF THE BUILDING. EXTERIOR. MORNING.

Césarin, coming in from the street, passes little Christophe, who is walking out with his schoolbag.

CÉSARIN: Hello, Christophe. Going to school? No strike on today?

A delivery man goes over to the café door, which is still closed.

CÉSARIN: Hello, Marcel.
MARCEL: How are things?
CÉSARIN: You're an early bird, aren't you?
MARCEL: It's cold.
CÉSARIN: You ought to have your own set of keys. [*He takes them from a ledge above the door.*] Anyway, they're right here. Give me a hand, will you? [*Césarin opens the shutters and the door.*] Come on, get a move on, Marcel. Give me that!

On the other side of the yard the concierge is hauling her garbage pails out. The Sanitation Department employee stops by for a chat.

S.D. EMPLOYEE: These garbage cans don't make any noise.
CONCIERGE: No, the new management got them. They're plastic.
S.D. EMPLOYEE: With wheels?
CONCIERGE: No . . . they're just noiseless.

The Sanitation Department employee moves on. In his corner of the courtyard Antoine is opening shop and taking the flowers out as the recluse looks on from his first-floor window.

THE RECLUSE: You seem a little nervous this morning.
ANTOINE: I am! I'm testing a new process I've invented. If it works, I'll get absolutely pure red. If it *doesn't*, I'd better start reading the want ads!

As he's about to go back into the shed, Ginette comes up to him.

GINETTE: Hey, Antoine, I looked up our horoscope. It's very favorable. Something big is going to happen to you and me.

Antoine, holding a rubber syringe and a plastic tube, goes over to the white carnations and carefully pours a product into the bucket of flowers. To his alarm, the bouquet lets out a sizzling cloud of white smoke.

ANTOINE: Damn, I guess I used too much . . . I think . . . [He looks up toward the recluse.] What do you think?
THE RECLUSE (throwing a newspaper down to him): I think you'd better start reading the want ads.

All that's left of the smoldering bouquet are a few carnations, burned to a crisp.

HYDRAULIC PLANT. EXTERIOR. DAY.
Against the background of a very modern building, a voice is heard reading the want ads.

VOICE (off): Major American hydraulic company, recently established in Paris, seeks dynamic, English-speaking young man. Rapid promotion.

HYDRAULIC PLANT. INTERIOR. DAY.
The elevator doors slide noiselessly open to make way for Antoine and another young man. They cross the hall to sit down on either end of an upholstered bench in the waiting room. Antoine seems tense; after a few minutes he gets up and heads for the rest rooms. As he is about to open one of the two doors, he notices that it's marked "Ladies." He steps into the one marked "Men."
Meanwhile, the other applicant takes a letter out of his pocket and reads it.

VOICE (off): Dear Sir: I wish to recommend to your kind attention the son of my old friend Baumel. This young man has distinguished himself in the Scout Movement and is a member of the Young Patriots. A loyal Frenchman, he is completely fluent in the language of Shakespeare. His dynamism would be of great value to a large American firm like yours.

The young man with connections puts his letter back in the envelope. A well-groomed blonde (Monique) emerges from the ladies' room.

THE YOUNG MAN WITH CONNECTIONS: Excuse me, mademoiselle. I believe I have an appointment with the director. Could you give him the letter, please?
MONIQUE: All right.
THE YOUNG MAN WITH CONNECTIONS: Thank you very much.

Monique heads for the office; the young man sits down to wait. Antoine comes out of the men's room and goes back to his seat. Now the young man with connections disappears into the men's room while Antoine waits on the bench. A second secretary (Nicole) goes over to him.

NICOLE: The director will see you now. Follow me.

PERSONNEL OFFICE. INTERIOR. DAY.
Nicole steps into the office, followed by Antoine.

NICOLE: Would you wait here, please. [Nicole walks over to one of the employees (the wise guy).] Can you tell Mr. Max that the applicant is here.
THE WISE GUY: Say hello first!
NICOLE: Hello! Now, hurry up.
THE WISE GUY (picking up the phone): Mr. Max, please. [To Nicole.] You look like a cream puff today. [With his free hand he caresses her breasts.]
NICOLE: Down, boy!

THE WISE GUY (*into the phone*): Mr. Max . . . yes, he's here. Yes, sir.

As Nicole and Antoine walk out of the personnel office, the wise guy calls out to her.

THE WISE GUY: Watch out, because I love cream puffs! [*Sitting back in his chair, he sighs.*] If I had a pair of breasts, I'd fondle them all day long.

THE DIRECTOR'S OFFICE. INTERIOR. DAY.
Antoine stands respectfully at attention as Mr. Max finishes reading the letter.

MR. MAX: This letter says some very nice things about you. You speak . . . [*He is interrupted by Monique, who has walked up to his desk.*]
MONIQUE: Mr. Max . . .
MR. MAX: Just a minute . . . [*To Antoine.*] You speak English well?
ANTOINE: A little.
MR. MAX (*to Monique*): Just a minute. [*He addresses Antoine in English.*] Speak to me in English.
ANTOINE (*answers in faltering English*): I speak a little, but I need practice.
MR. MAX: You read it better than you speak it. [*In English.*] Do you read American newspapers?
ANTOINE (*his English sounds more confident as he recites*): I prefer poetry to prose.

A little nonplussed, Mr. Max steals a glance at the letter he's holding in his hand. Monique takes advantage of the pause to speak up.

MONIQUE: Mr. Max, I believe there is a mistake.
MR. MAX (*speaking in English*): Look, leave us alone, will you. I'll call you when I need you.

As soon as Monique has left the office Mr. Max addresses Antoine in French again.

MR. MAX: Well . . . the problem for our employees here is transportation. Do you have a car?
ANTOINE (*in English*): I am not in a hurry. I prefer to cross the town.
MR. MAX (*looking puzzled*): Yeah . . . [*but deciding to trust him*] well, you can't start at the top, of course, but I can put you on the scale models. [*Back to English.*] Come on over here to the window. I wanna show you something. [*Antoine steps over to the window.*] It's impressive, isn't it?

While Mr. Max points to the park outside the window, Antoine raises his eyes toward the sky.

ANTOINE (*reciting in English*): The birds fly high in the sky.
MR. MAX: No, no. Look down there. We've set up a model of a harbor, with port installations. You'll maneuver the boats . . . [*He beams at Antoine.*] D'you like the job?
ANTOINE: I like it very much.
MR. MAX: Good. You'll see. My employees are so happy here that they hate to stay home on Sundays!
ANTOINE (*solemnly*): Really?

HYDRAULIC PLANT. EXTERIOR. DAY.
A scale model of a port installation, including a water basin, with a few miniature boats. The wise guy is showing Antoine the ropes.

THE WISE GUY: This is what the port will be like according to the plans. For the time being, the harbor silts up, so we've built a dike from here to there. Otherwise, it's accurate to scale. [*He shows him a tele-guiding apparatus.*] Your job will be to run the boats by remote control. See, you press the button and away they go! D'you like the job? [*He imitates Mr. Max's American accent.*] "You'll see. My employees are so happy here that they hate to stay home on Sundays!" Did he pull that one on you? He says that to all the new ones!

BEDROOM OF THE DOINEL APARTMENT. INTERIOR. EVENING.

Antoine and Christine are in bed; she's reading a book and he's reading a newspaper.

ANTOINE: They've got their nerve . . . printing that in the paper!
CHRISTINE: What?
ANTOINE: Listen: it's about the Common Market . . . in Brussels. [*He reads out loud.*] "The session was resumed at eight o'clock and adjourned at midnight. Back in their hotel rooms, the delegates were rewarded by a lascivious broad."
CHRISTINE: That's incredible!
ANTOINE: Look, it's right here. Imagine . . . in *Le Monde!* Listen: "The session was resumed at eight o'clock and adjourned at midnight. Back in their hotel rooms, the delegates were rewarded by a lascivious broad."
CHRISTINE: I don't believe you!
ANTOINE: Well, read it yourself!
CHRISTINE (*reading*): "The session was resumed at eight o'clock and adjourned at midnight. Back in their hotel rooms, the delegates were rewarded by a lavish smorgasbord." You liar! [*They both laugh.*]
ANTOINE: Lights out. [*They continue to talk in the darkness.*] I had you going there, didn't I?

CHRISTINE: Yes.
ANTOINE: Look, tomorrow morning remind me that I've got to tell you something very important.
CHRISTINE: What?
ANTOINE: I'll tell you tomorrow.
CHRISTINE: Why not now?
ANTOINE: Because you couldn't sleep.

KITCHEN OF THE DOINEL APARTMENT. INTERIOR. DAY.

Christine is grinding the coffee. Antoine's voice is heard off.

ANTOINE: Christine! Christine!
CHRISTINE: What is it?

She puts the grinder down and opens the kitchen window, which faces the bathroom window across the courtyard. Antoine is at the bathroom window, a toothbrush in one hand and an empty tube of tooth paste in the other which he waves at Christine.

CHRISTINE: Oh, yes, I bought some. Wait. [She picks up a tube from the top of the frigidaire and, after unwrapping it, goes back to the window to show it to Antoine.] It's a new brand.

Antoine looks back apprehensively. Christine throws the tube over and he catches it. She raises her thumb.

CHRISTINE: First-class!

Antoine grimaces his appreciation before going back to the sink.

PARIS STREET. EXTERIOR. DAY.

Antoine and Christine are walking along the street together. Suddenly he sees his friend, the moocher. Muttering an explanation, he tries to hide behind Christine.

ANTOINE: Damn! There's a guy I know. He owes me thirty francs . . . he'll be embarrassed. Hide me.

But the moocher has spotted Antoine.

THE MOOCHER: Hi, Doinel, how are things?
ANTOINE: Hi. I'm all right.
THE MOOCHER: Say, I owe you thirty francs, right?
ANTOINE: Yeah, but it doesn't . . .
THE MOOCHER: Look, if you let me have twenty more, that'll make it an even fifty. You'll get it all back at once.
ANTOINE: Oh, fine! [*He gives him the money.*]
THE MOOCHER: How're things?
ANTOINE: All right. Well, so long.
THE MOOCHER: Thanks. So long.
ANTOINE: I'll see you around!

The moocher goes on his way while Antoine catches up with Christine, who has observed the scene with a smile from a little distance away. They resume their walk. Christine stops in front of a building.

CHRISTINE: Well, you'd better leave me here.
ANTOINE: Where's your violin?
CHRISTINE: I'm not giving a lesson.
ANTOINE: Well, where are you going?
CHRISTINE (*playfully*): Do you always tell me where you go? I'll see you tonight.

She goes into the building. Antoine looks over the directory
outside and sees:

Maître Bacquet, Notary Public—1st floor

Doctor Magori, Gynecologist—5th floor

Madame Chevalier, Dressmaker—3rd floor

He walks off.

SUBWAY PLATFORM. INTERIOR. DAY.

Antoine, walking along the platform, passes a huge poster advertising "Baby Comfort." He pays no attention to it, but we remain on the poster. Suddenly he turns back and stops to stare at the poster, which features a beautiful, smiling baby. He runs over to the turnstile, but the arrival of a train causes it to shut automatically. He can't get out. He goes back to the poster and stares at it thoughtfully.

PLACE CLICHY. EXTERIOR. DAY.

Antoine buys a record. The label on the jacket reads: "Natural Childbirth."

THE DOINEL APARTMENT. INTERIOR. DAY.

The record playing on the pickup gives medical instruction on "Natural Childbirth."

VOICE: Watch out for the contraction . . . short breaths . . . keep going! Keep it up, keep it up, very good . . .

STAIRCASE OF THE DOINEL APARTMENT HOUSE. INTERIOR. DAY.

We still hear the medical instructions on the record. The parking agent coming down the stairs and an elderly lady walking up stop to listen. They exchange a meaningful look.

THE DARBON VILLA. EXTERIOR. DAY.

Antoine and Christine, she now in a very advanced stage of her pregnancy, are taking their leave. The indistinct conversation with her parents consists of admonitions—"Take care of her and call me if there's anything I can do"—and reassurances—"Of course. Don't worry." After a final round of kisses the young couple crosses the garden, hand in hand, heading for the street.

THE BUILDING COURTYARD. EXTERIOR. DAY.

Antoine and Christine, tender and smiling, are coming into the courtyard. He caresses her stomach. As they pass the concierge's loge, she stops them.

CONCIERGE: Madame Doinel, I've got something for you. [*She hands her an envelope.*] It's some advertising from the maternity shop, I think.

Césarin and the Sanitation Department employee are at the café window.

ANTOINE: Hello, Césarin.
CHRISTINE: Hello.
CÉSARIN: Hello, folks.

Antoine and Christine disappear through the doorway of the building.

S.D. EMPLOYEE: Say, it looks like Madame Doinel got stung by a mosquito.
CÉSARIN: That was some mosquito! [*The two men laugh together, but Césarin suddenly comes to attention.*] Look! The strangler!

They assume an air of indifference as Monsieur X passes in front of them. As soon as he's out of sight, Césarin speaks up.

CÉSARIN: He looks mean! [*His friend nods in agreement.*]

BUILDING STAIRWAY. INTERIOR. DAY.

On their way up, Antoine and Christine pass their neighbor, the tenor, who greets them formally by sweeping off his hat. A woman's voice calls down.

TENOR'S WIFE (off): I'm coming, dear!

A few steps ahead, on the staircase, is a fur coat and a purse. The tenor's wife hurries down and Christine picks up the coat.

CHRISTINE: Here, let me help you.

Antoine hands the woman her purse.

TENOR'S WIFE: Thank you very much. [*She puts her hand on Christine's stomach.*] It won't be long now, will it? You're so lucky! [*She disappears down the stairs.*]

PERSONNEL OFFICE AT THE HYDRAULIC PLANT.
INTERIOR. DAY.
The phone rings; a young employee picks it up.

THE EMPLOYEE: Monsieur Doinel? He's not here.

Just as he's about to hang up, Nicole takes the receiver from him.

NICOLE: Wait a minute. [*Into the phone.*] The hospital? No, but I'll give him the message. Is it a girl or a boy?

HYDRAULIC PLANT GARDEN. EXTERIOR. EVENING.
Hurrying across the garden, Nicole reaches a small bridge over the water basin. Antoine's voice can be heard in the distance.

ANTOINE (*off*): Hey, Mr. Max . . . a little farther over . . . that boat over there . . . That's it . . . very good.
NICOLE (*shouting*): Antoine! Antoine!

He is too far away to hear her. She holds up a magazine featuring the pictures of a little boy and a little girl. She points to one of the children. Antoine adjusts the lens of the camera he's holding and peers into it: she's pointing toward the boy!

CLINIC. EXTERIOR. NIGHT.

Antoine, running toward the clinic, meets his in-laws, who are coming out.

DARBON: Congratulations, Antoine!
MME. DARBON: Bravo . . . it's a lovely little boy. I'm so pleased, he's under the sign of Aquarius.
DARBON: I'd say he was in the arms of Morpheus!
MME. DARBON: Do you want to have dinner with us?
ANTOINE: No, not tonight. I'll stay with Christine.
DARBON (to his wife): Don't hold him up. [To Antoine.] Go on . . . she's waiting.
MME. DARBON: Good-bye.
DARBON: Good-bye. [M. and Mme. Darbon head for their car.]
MME. DARBON: He could have brought her a few flowers!
DARBON: He only found out three-quarters of an hour ago at the office . . . he ran right over . . . there was no time. Listen, let's get them that extra room next door. They can knock out the wall . . . it'll be perfect. What do you think?

CLINIC. CHRISTINE'S ROOM. INTERIOR. EVENING.

Christine is in bed.

CHRISTINE: Be careful . . . hold his head up.

Now we discover Antoine holding the infant in his arms.

ANTOINE: What a wonderful child. He's really fantastic! [He walks up and down the room.] I was sure he would be, but he's even more wonderful than I thought. He'll be the writer I wanted to be—Victor Hugo or nothing! [He speaks to the baby.] What Napoleon did with the sword, you'll do with the pen. [To Christine.] Did you notice? When I picked him up, he smiled at me!

CHRISTINE: You're crazy! Babies only smile after three weeks!
ANTOINE: Well, he smiled at me!

There is a knock at the door.

CHRISTINE: Come in.

A nurse opens the door.

THE NURSE: A photographer is making the rounds. Would you like him to take a picture?
CHRISTINE: I'm too tired now . . . some other time.
ANTOINE: Well, I'm not one bit tired. Send him in.

The photographer appears. Close-up of Antoine holding the baby and looking very moved. The photographer takes the picture. Antoine beams with pride.

There is a quick cut of a nurse walking down the corridor; then we go back to Christine's room. Antoine is sitting on the edge of the bed. Christine seems tired and a little remote.

CHRISTINE: I'd like to be by myself now.
ANTOINE: You would?
CHRISTINE: You can eat with my parents.
ANTOINE: They asked me a few minutes ago. I turned them down to stay with you. I can tell you a story, or we can listen to some music on the radio if you like . . .
CHRISTINE (abruptly): Go away!
ANTOINE (nonplussed): Go away!
CHRISTINE (more gently): Yes . . . please.
ANTOINE: Whatever you say. [He kisses her hand.] See you tomorrow. [He gets up to leave. At the door he turns around for a last try.] On a night like this I didn't want you to be all by yourself.
CHRISTINE: I waited for that child all by myself.

A CAFETERIA. EXTERIOR. NIGHT.
   The neon sign of a cafeteria. Through the window we see Antoine having a solitary meal.

A STREET. EXTERIOR. NIGHT.
   Antoine, walking alone, notices his friend, the moocher. He turns back to speak to him.

ANTOINE: Say, Jacques, how are you?
THE MOOCHER: Hi, what's new?
ANTOINE: I'm glad to see you, fellow. Good news: I'm a father!
THE MOOCHER: Christ!
ANTOINE: Yes, it's a boy.
THE MOOCHER: You're happy, then?
ANTOINE: And how!

THE MOOCHER: Say, I owe you fifty, right?

ANTOINE: I guess so . . .

THE MOOCHER: Well, if you can let me have fifty more that'd be an even hundred. I'll pay you the lump sum.

ANTOINE: Certainly . . . with pleasure . . . it's perfectly all right.

THE MOOCHER: Christ, you must be real happy.

ANTOINE (*handing him the money*): I'm elated, really wild with joy!

THE MOOCHER: Well, so long.

ANTOINE: Good-bye.

The two men go off on their separate ways. Noticing a phone booth, Antoine turns back to it and goes inside to dial a number.

ANTOINE: Hello . . . Can I speak to Jean . . . Oh, hello, Madame Eustache. Could I speak to Jean, please? Oh! Well, look . . . can you tell him that Antoine Doinel is a father. That's it . . . tell him that Antoine had a little boy . . . yes, it's a boy . . . Thank you very much. And don't forget to give him the message. Good-bye, madame. [*He hangs up and goes on his way.*]

CLINIC. CHRISTINE'S ROOM. INTERIOR. EVENING.

Christine is in bed with the baby in her arms. Antoine is seated on a corner of the bed.

CHRISTINE: Don't forget, Antoine, you must register his birth to-morrow. We've got to decide now. I've been thinking it over. I prefer Ghislain.

ANTOINE: Ghislain . . . it sounds pretentious . . . sissified.

CHRISTINE: Well, have you got a better idea?

ANTOINE: I like Alphonse. It's just right.

CHRISTINE: Alphonse is for peasants . . . besides, Ghislain is the name of my mother's brother.

CITY HALL. INTERIOR. DAY.

An employee is making out the birth certificate as Antoine faces her on the other side of the counter window.

EMPLOYEE: Mother: Christine Doinel. What is the baby's name?
ANTOINE (*making up his mind*): Alphonse!

THE BUILDING COURTYARD. EXTERIOR. DAY.

On his way in, Antoine is intercepted by Césarin.

CÉSARIN: How'd it go?
ANTOINE: I'm very happy.
CÉSARIN: A boy?
ANTOINE: Yes, it's a boy.
CÉSARIN: Congratulations!
THE CONCIERGE: It's a little boy? Congratulations! How'd it go?
S.D. EMPLOYEE: Well?
ANTOINE: It was difficult at first.
CÉSARIN: Is that so?
ANTOINE: But she's fine now . . . she's in good shape.
CÉSARIN: Good.
CONCIERGE: Well, that's just fine. Congratulations!
S.D. EMPLOYEE: Bravo!

Ginette, carrying a crate of wine bottles, moves over to the group.

GINETTE: Antoine, give me a hand.
ANTOINE: Sure. [*He apologizes to the men, picks up the crate and follows Ginette.*] I'm glad . . . it's a boy.
CÉSARIN (*off*): Yes, very good.

GINETTE: Your wife will have to stay in the clinic for another week, won't she?

ANTOINE: Yes, for another week.

GINETTE: Listen . . .

ANTOINE: What . . .

GINETTE: You must be lonely up there, all by yourself in bed, the whole night long . . .

ANTOINE: No, no, I'm fine. [*Antoine walks back to the men.*]

CÉSARIN: Is he cute?

ANTOINE: Yes, he's all pink . . .

CÉSARIN: Is that so?

ANTOINE: And his hands are tiny.

A TENANT: How are you? Congratulations on the blessed event!

CÉSARIN: Are his eyes open yet?

ANTOINE: Yes . . . his eyes are . . . he has an extraordinary look . . .

S.D. EMPLOYEE: What about hair? Has he got any hair?

ANTOINE: Yes, yes, he's all curly.

S.D. EMPLOYEE: Who does he look like?

CÉSARIN (*interrupting them*): Shhhhh! [*The group stands aside to allow the strangler to pass through.*] Watch out for him. There've been lots of kidnappings lately. [*The group watches the strangler moving off.*]

S.D. EMPLOYEE (*off*): The strangler . . .

CONCIERGE (*off*): That's what we call him too . . .

GINETTE: Don't stare like that, he'll notice it!

CÉSARIN: She's right. Come inside! [*He urges them all inside the café.*] Drinks on the house!

S.D. EMPLOYEE: On the house?

CÉSARIN: That's right.

S.D. EMPLOYEE: Your treat?

CÉSARIN: On me!

S.D. EMPLOYEE: Well, this is really a blessed event!

CÉSARIN: You're all my guests! [*Turning to the parking agent who's just walked in.*] Everybody, even you!

DOINEL APARTMENT. INTERIOR. DAY.
    Christine and Sylvana, the tenor's wife, are watching Antoine knock down the wall that divides their apartment from the extra room. Antoine, on the other side of the wall, can be seen through the hole. He stops hammering.

ANTOINE: All right?
CHRISTINE: All right.
ANTOINE: Then I'll go on.

    He resumes his hammering, while the two women laughingly hop around to avoid the falling debris.

CHRISTINE: Look out, Sylvana . . . [*The whole side of the wall collapses.*] Oh, terrific!

BUILDING STAIRCASE. INTERIOR. DAY.
    Two tenants on the stairway appear to be rather intrigued by all the shouting and noise inside the Doinel apartment.

DOINEL APARTMENT. INTERIOR. DAY.
    The wall is practically demolished now. Antoine helps Sylvana and Christine climb over the debris, into the extra room, the walls of which are lined with old newspapers.

ANTOINE: There, it's done, Sylvana. [*He helps her in.*]
SYLVANA (*laughingly*): You have to be in shape, right?
ANTOINE (*carefully holding her*): All right now?
SYLVANA: Terrific!
CHRISTINE: It is.
ANTOINE: Do you like it, Sylvana?
SYLVANA: It's wonderful.
ANTOINE: This'll be our room.

SYLVANA: And there, in the morning . . .
ANTOINE: No street noises here.
SYLVANA (*points to the window*): I can wave from my window . . . it's right nearby.
ANTOINE: Yes! The baby's room will be over there.
SYLVANA: I see.
CHRISTINE: It'll work out very well.
ANTOINE: So you like it, Sylvana? [*He whirls her around.*]
SYLVANA: Wonderful.

The inspection is over; Antoine helps the two women back to the other side of the wall, inside the Doinel apartment.

ANTOINE: Careful . . .
SYLVANA: All right.
ANTOINE: Go ahead, Christine.

Christine and Antoine show Sylvana to the door.

SYLVANA: Good-bye now. I've got to get my dinner ready.
ANTOINE: Good-bye, Sylvana. See you soon.
CHRISTINE: Good-bye, Sylvana.
SYLVANA: Good-bye.

After she leaves, Christine's smile disappears.

CHRISTINE: I saw you!
ANTOINE: What did you see?
CHRISTINE: I'm not blind, you know. You go for her, don't you?
ANTOINE: Who are you talking about?
CHRISTINE: Sylvana. Don't try to deny it. You go for her.
ANTOINE: No, I don't.

Throughout this dialogue, Christine pummels Antoine with her fists, while he laughingly tries to protect himself.

CHRISTINE: Yeah . . . A nice plump Italian . . . with beautiful breasts . . . a sexy mouth . . . and everything!
ANTOINE: No!
CHRISTINE: Yes!
ANTOINE: No . . . honestly!
CHRISTINE: Yes, yes, yes!
ANTOINE: No!
CHRISTINE: Yes . . . you bastard!

Antoine, still walking backward to avoid the blows, trips over the debris and disappears in the hole that separates the two rooms.

BEDROOM. INTERIOR. EVENING.
Antoine and Christine are in bed. They exchange a few gentle kisses.

ANTOINE: Do you remember the first time we kissed?
CHRISTINE: Yes, I was too petrified to move.
ANTOINE: What are you talking about? You did it all!
CHRISTINE: Oh, no, I didn't. You're mistaken . . .
ANTOINE: Not at all, I remember very well! We were in a cab and it stopped. I leaned over to give you a little peck on the cheek, just to say good-bye. And I saw you parting your lips, so I said to myself: "This is it, she wants me to really kiss her!"
CHRISTINE: You're out of your mind!
ANTOINE: Certainly not! I am not saying I didn't enjoy it, but just that you're the one who took the initiative.
CHRISTINE: That's your story! The truth is that you grabbed me . . . and I let you.
ANTOINE: Honestly, it wasn't that way at all. I remember it very clearly. This is just the way you were . . . your head thrown back, your eyes closed, your lips slightly open . . . Here, I'll show you. [He does.]

Christine laughs.

ANTOINE: You had it all worked out in your mind. You'd thought about it, hadn't you?
CHRISTINE: Thought about what?
ANTOINE: About you and me kissing one day.
CHRISTINE: Well naturally, all girls think about that.
ANTOINE: They do, huh? So you admit it!

Christine laughs.

THE BUILDING COURTYARD. EXTERIOR. DAY.
Christine, carrying her violin case, knocks at the concierge's loge.

CHRISTINE: Good morning, Madame Martin. I'll take Ghislain now.
CONCIERGE: He was very good. He didn't cry once.
CHRISTINE: If he keeps on being so good, I'll be able to work at home again.
CONCIERGE: Here he is.
CHRISTINE: How's my boy?
CONCIERGE: There's some mail for you . . . where is it? . . . It's a certificate.

The baby in one arm, the violin case in the other, Christine motions to the concierge to open the envelope.

CONCIERGE (after reading): You named him Alphonse?
CHRISTINE: Alphonse? What do you mean?
CONCIERGE: Look, it says so here: Alphonse.
CHRISTINE: Antoine did that. He won't get away with it. He knew I didn't want that name!

The concierge slides the envelope into Christine's pocket. As Christine heads for the building, the parking agent, who has been watching from the café window, comes out into the courtyard for a better look at the comely young woman.

PARKING AGENT (*muttering to himself*): I'd lay her badly, but I'd lay her gladly!

THE BABY'S ROOM IN THE DOINEL APARTMENT.
INTERIOR. DAY.
     Antoine is playing with Alphonse, while Christine is putting the baby's things away in the closet.

ANTOINE: Alphonse'll be a great writer. You know what I'm going to do? I'll educate him myself. He won't go to school . . . That way, he'll learn only the important things!
CHRISTINE: Well, we'll see about that later. [*She comes over to pick the baby up.*] Come on, my little Ghislain, come baby . . .
ANTOINE: Alphonse!
CHRISTINE: Come on, Ghislain. [*She undresses the baby.*] Oh, what a pretty little bottom!
ANTOINE: Alphonse has a pretty little bottom . . . just like his mother.
CHRISTINE (*leaning over the baby*): Yes, Ghislain, look, that's it . . . [*She stands up with the baby in her arms, looking over at Antoine.*] Look at Papa. He's going to the bathroom. He's getting ready as if for an arctic expedition . . . see . . . the flashlight . . . a book . . . a knife to cut the pages . . . Now what? Oh, the newspaper!

Antoine, having assembled all of the objects she's mentioned, now heads for the bathroom.

DOINEL APARTMENT. EXTERIOR. LATE AFTERNOON.

During the following dialogue, the camera pans back and forth from Christine, at the kitchen window, to Antoine, at the bathroom window.

CHRISTINE: Antoine! You forgot to go shopping?
ANTOINE: For what?
CHRISTINE: I left the list on the table.
ANTOINE: For what?
CHRISTINE: I left the list on the table.
ANTOINE: You left me a list?
CHRISTINE: Yes.
ANTOINE: I didn't notice it.
CHRISTINE: Well, there's nothing here.
ANTOINE: Nothing to eat?
CHRISTINE: I wrote it all down for you.
ANTOINE: Listen, let's ask Madame Martin to baby-sit. We'll go out.
CHRISTINE: She's not home this evening.
ANTOINE: Isn't there anything in the frigidaire?
CHRISTINE: This baby food is all there is.
ANTOINE: Yummy! It looks delicious. Let's eat that.
CHRISTINE: You mean it?
ANTOINE: Certainly.
CHRISTINE: What if he wakes up?
ANTOINE: Who, Alphonse? You know he never wakes up! We'll buy him some more in the morning. Tonight, we eat.
CHRISTINE: Okay.

DOINEL DINING ROOM. INTERIOR. EVENING.

Antoine and Christine are eating Alphonse's baby food and looking at television. The announcer is introducing the program.

VOICE (off): At the theater: Tonight, straight from Marienbad.

The performer appears on the screen.

CHRISTINE: Look! It's our neighbor . . . the strangler!
THE STRANGLER: Hello, hello . . . I'm listening.
CHRISTINE: Did you know he was a professional entertainer?
ANTOINE: No, I didn't. Is he a singer?
CHRISTINE: No, he does impersonations.
THE STRANGLER: Alexandre Alexandrovich . . . we met last year
and you kept an old picture of me . . .
CHRISTINE: He's not bad.
THE STRANGLER: Wait . . .
CHRISTINE: Look . . . he's great!
ANTOINE: Yeah.
THE STRANGLER: Last year . . . it was in Carlsbad . . . or perhaps
in Marienbad . . . Once again, I walk through the drawing rooms
. . . through the long corridors . . . luxurious, lugubrious. I am
not an apparition, I am a woman, which is just the opposite. You
say that I am exceptional. That's true, I *am* exceptional.

At this, Christine laughs out loud, but Antoine seems a little
put out.

BUILDING COURTYARD. EXTERIOR. MORNING.
The strangler, coming out of the building, is intercepted by
Ginette. The concierge and several of the tenants come over to
congratulate him.

GINETTE: We saw you last night!
CONCIERGE: I saw you too.
TENANT: You were terrific!
CONCIERGE: I recognized you right away.
THE RECLUSE (*from his window*): You're a sly one, aren't you.
You didn't tell us you were a comedian.
GINETTE: I recognized you at once.

THE WHOLE GROUP: So did I. Me too. Congratulations!

Little Christophe, on his way to school, and Antoine, on his way to work, also stop by to congratulate the strangler.

HYDRAULIC PLANT. THE BASIN. EXTERIOR. DAY.

Antoine is maneuvering his boats around the basin. Mr. Max and Monique, followed by two Japanese men in business suits and two Japanese women in traditional costume, are heading toward him.

MR. MAX (*in English*): Now, Mr. Doinel . . . this is . . . you met . . . this is Mrs. Yamada, Mr. Yamada, Miss Yamada. [*He turns to the Japanese family.*] He makes the boats go around . . . manipulate . . . understand?

The younger man, who is probably Mr. Yamada's secretary, translates what Mr. Max is saying.

MR. MAX (*to Antoine*): Can you maneuver the boats, please? Thanks.

Mr. Max launches on a series of technical explanations, which the secretary translates to his boss. During this conversation, the camera remains on Antoine and Mlle. Kyoko Yamada, who appear to be very interested in each other.

Kyoko steps over to whisper something in Mme. Yamada's ear; she whispers something to her husband, who whispers something to his secretary, who whispers to Mr. Max, who finally whispers the request to Antoine. Antoine goes up to Kyoko, who nods, and both of them head for the building of the Hydraulic Plant.

HYDRAULIC PLANT. ELEVATOR. INTERIOR. DAY.
Inside the elevator Antoine and Kyoko eye each other as she toys with her bracelet.

HYDRAULIC PLANT HALLWAY. INTERIOR. DAY.
Coming out of the elevator, Antoine and Kyoko run into the office wise guy, who has just stepped out of an office.

WISE GUY: Hi, Doinel. Need any help?

Antoine directs the young girl toward a door marked "Ladies."

HYDRAULIC PLANT. THE BASIN. EXTERIOR. DAY.
The little boats are circling around the basin. Kyoko, under Antoine's amused look, is maneuvering them. Suddenly her bracelet falls into the water. Antoine notices it, but before he can retrieve it, Yamada calls his daughter to join the rest of the group that is drinking champagne with Mr. Max.

MR. MAX: Sayonara! Sayonara! Okay? Sayonara, Monique! Sayonara, Madame! Contract! *Beaucoup* dollars! Right! Champagne . . . *Champagne américain!* Here we go! [*They empty their glasses.*]

The title across the screen reads: "The following morning."

HYDRAULIC PLANT. THE BASIN. EXTERIOR. DAY.
The wise guy, on his way to work, stops at the bridge and looks perplexed as he sees Antoine leaning over and fishing for something inside the basin.

LANDING AND KYOKO APARTMENT. INTERIOR.
EVENING.

Antoine knocks at the door. Kyoko opens it.

KYOKO: Sir?
ANTOINE: Hello. Remember me? I work at the Hydraulic Plant.
KYOKO: Oh, hello.
ANTOINE: I came . . . I brought you something.
KYOKO: Come in.

She closes the door behind him. Antoine hands her a little
package which she opens. It is her bracelet.

KYOKO: You noticed that I lost it?
ANTOINE: I saw it fall into the water and . . . I was surprised that
you didn't say anything.
KYOKO: Well, the American gentleman mentioned that the model
was very fragile and I . . . I was sorry about the bracelet, but I
didn't want to bother you.
ANTOINE: I thought you'd be glad to have it again.
KYOKO: Thank you very much. Come in.

She takes him inside the room. Antoine now sees another
Japanese girl, in traditional garb, seated on her heels at a low table.

KYOKO: Monsieur . . . ?
ANTOINE: Doinel.
KYOKO: Monsieur Doinel . . . Mademoiselle Maki, my roommate.

Kyoko sits down next to her friend. The two of them converse
while the friend attaches the bracelet to Kyoko's wrist. Antoine, a
little intimidated by this conversation he does not understand, walks
around the room. Kyoko gets up and goes over to him.

KYOKO: Won't you sit down.

ANTOINE: I'm sorry, but I have to go . . . I'm already . . .
KYOKO: We were just having tea . . . If you'd like . . .
ANTOINE: I'd love to, but I'm already late. I've got to go now.
KYOKO: I see.
ANTOINE (*heading for the door*): I hope you'll excuse me.

Kyoko opens the door for him.

ANTOINE: All right then . . .
KYOKO: I'll show you out. [*She takes him to the stairs.*]
ANTOINE: Good day, mademoiselle.

Antoine reaches out for a handshake. To his surprise, Kyoko puts her arms around his neck and kisses him on the mouth. She goes back into her apartment while Antoine goes down the stairs looking bemused.

BUILDING COURTYARD. EXTERIOR. EVENING.
Antoine, coming home, is intercepted by Césarin, who's closing the café.

CÉSARIN: Good evening, Antoine.
ANTOINE: How are things?
CÉSARIN: We never see you anymore since you changed jobs. I hear you're working for the Americans. Do they pay in dollars?
ANTOINE: The thing is that it gives me time to think.
CÉSARIN: Is that so?
ANTOINE: Yes. I'm writing a novel.
CÉSARIN: No kidding!
ANTOINE: Don't mention it to my wife. I write at night, when she's asleep.
CÉSARIN: So you're a novelist. Like Baudelaire! He started with flowers too.
ANTOINE: Yes, but Baudelaire didn't write novels.

CÉSARIN: Is that so? How about *Flowers of Evil?*

ANTOINE: That's poetry.

CÉSARIN: I know more about him than you do . . . I just read an article on Baudelaire. Did you know his father was a priest?

ANTOINE: Baudelaire?

CÉSARIN: Absolutely. His father was an ordained priest; then he worked for a family . . . the Choiseul-Praslins . . . as a tutor for the children. [*Throughout this conversation Césarin is hauling bottles from the courtyard into the café.*] Would you open that door for me? . . . What is your novel about?

ANTOINE: You know . . . about life in general . . . my youth . . .

CÉSARIN: I see.

ANTOINE: I go from the particular to the general.

CÉSARIN: Is that so? We'll have to read it. I get an autographed copy, right?

ANTOINE: Yes. "For Césarin."

CÉSARIN: What's the title?

ANTOINE: I haven't got one yet.

CÉSARIN: It shouldn't be hard to find. Are there any trumpets in your novel?

ANTOINE: No.

CÉSARIN: Any drums?

ANTOINE: No.

CÉSARIN: Then you call it *With No Trumpets and No Drums!*

ANTOINE: That's an idea.

CÉSARIN: Not bad, huh?

ANTOINE: So long.

CÉSARIN: So long, ha, ha! [*Césarin suddenly notices a man staggering over in his direction.*] What's this . . . Oh, God . . . What do you want? [*Césarin grabs hold of the man, who's trying to go into the café, and manages to close the door.*] We're closed. What are you looking for?

THE MAN: I'm looking for a fight!

CÉSARIN (*dragging the man toward the street*): Oh, I see. Listen, be nice. This is just a little place . . . we cater to old folks and

children. You're not going to fight them, right? Be a good fellow
. . . If you want a fight, there's a café right nearby. Just turn right,
around the corner, and you'll get what you're looking for.

DOINEL BEDROOM. INTERIOR. EVENING.
    Antoine and Christine are in bed, reading. Christine is wear-
ing eyeglasses.

CHRISTINE (*leaning over to look at Antoine's book*): What are
you reading? *Japanese Women?*

ANTOINE: I need it for my work. [*Antoine leans over to Christine's book, titled* Nureyev, *then he looks at Christine.*] Let's see. Say, you look good in glasses.
CHRISTINE: Is that so? I wish I didn't need them.
ANTOINE: No, they look very good on you.

Christine removes her glasses, puts her book down and turns the light out. Antoine puts his book down.

ANTOINE: I've finished.
CHRISTINE: I know why you like glasses. *She* wore them, didn't she?
ANTOINE: Who?
CHRISTINE: Your first girl.
ANTOINE: No, she didn't wear glasses.
CHRISTINE: I thought she did.
ANTOINE: No.
CHRISTINE: She made you suffer, didn't she?
ANTOINE: You can say that again! She had me going in circles. What a nightmare that was! But you know something? I fell out of love in one hour! At eight P.M. I was wild about her and by nine P.M. I couldn't bear the sight of her. It was over. I was cured!
CHRISTINE: I suppose she said the wrong thing . . .
ANTOINE: Exactly. I don't even remember what she said, but it sure was a relief.

BABY'S ROOM. INTERIOR. NIGHT.
A quick cut of the baby, sleeping on his stomach.

DOINEL BEDROOM. INTERIOR. EVENING.
Back to Antoine and Christine.

ANTOINE: If I ask you something, will you do it?
CHRISTINE: It depends . . .

ANTOINE: You're quibbling again. Will you do it, yes or no?
CHRISTINE: It depends. Ask me.
ANTOINE: Would you put your glasses on again?

Christine puts her glasses on as the image fades out.

HYDRAULIC PLANT. THE BASIN. EXTERIOR. DAY.
A master shot of Antoine maneuvering his miniature boats in the basin.

LANDING AND KYOKO APARTMENT. INTERIOR. EVENING.
Antoine knocks at the door. Kyoko opens it and shows him in. She is wearing a miniskirt and a sweater.

KYOKO: Hello, Antoine.
ANTOINE: Hello, Kyoko. Am I too early?
KYOKO: Not at all. Come in.
ANTOINE: How are you?
KYOKO: Fine. And you?
ANTOINE: I'm fine.
KYOKO: What shall we do tonight? Do you have anything in mind?
ANTOINE: I thought we'd go to a movie. I brought the program guide, but I haven't picked one out yet.
KYOKO: You know, I thought we might have dinner here.
ANTOINE: That'd be fine.
KYOKO: We could go to a movie later on.
ANTOINE: Good idea.
KYOKO: Fine. Look over the program. I'll be right back.

Antoine opens the guide, furtively looking toward the next room, where Kyoko is talking to Mlle. Maki, her roommate. It is clear that a heated discussion is taking place; both girls circle nervously around the room, as Antoine watches their legs. On his left, the low table has been set for two. The conversation next door comes to an end. Kyoko curtly hands her friend her coat and purse, then comes back to Antoine.

KYOKO: My friend wants to apologize. Her mother is very ill and she can't stay with us.
ANTOINE: Really? I hope it's not too serious.
KYOKO: Yes, her mother's very sick . . . she has to leave right away.

Mlle. Maki heads for the door and then down the stairs. As soon as she is out of sight, Kyoko opens the door; after making sure her friend has gone, she hangs a little Japanese sign on the door before closing it again. The camera pans over to the sign which reads: "Do Not Disturb."

DOINEL APARTMENT. INTERIOR. NIGHT.
    Antoine comes in, closing the door behind him softly, and steals through the dark hallway into the kitchen, where he switches the light on. He then goes into his room, picks up his pajamas and heads back for the kitchen. The bedroom suddenly lights up.

CHRISTINE: Is that you, Antoine? Isn't it rather late?
ANTOINE: We worked late this evening.
CHRISTINE: Look at the time!
ANTOINE: I had to eat, didn't I?

DOINEL BEDROOM. INTERIOR. DAY.
    Christine, at the window, is speaking to Sylvana across the courtyard, at the window of her own apartment.

CHRISTINE: He tiptoes in, in the darkness. He assumes I'm fast asleep. I look at the clock: three A.M.! When I ask for an explanation, you know what he says? "I had to eat, didn't I?"

Sylvana is all ears.

KYOKO'S APARTMENT. INTERIOR. EVENING.

We see four small handwritten notes, each one on a different color paper. A hand picks up one of them. The camera moves back to show Kyoko rolling it tightly and inserting it in a box filled with tulips. We hear her voice off.

KYOKO (off): Kyoko loves Antoine.
             Come when you can, but come soon.
             She says good night and thinks of Antoine.

HYDRAULIC PLANT PERSONNEL OFFICE. INTERIOR. DAY.

An employee walks in carrying a bouquet of tulips in a transparent plastic box. He takes them over to the manager's desk.

THE EMPLOYEE: The doorman gave it to me!
THE MANAGER: What is it? Who's it for?
THE EMPLOYEE: I don't know. He didn't say anything.
THE.MANAGER (handing the box to Monique): It must be for you.
MONIQUE: No. Nobody would send me flowers here. They must be for Nicole.
NICOLE: I don't know . . . Wait! Maybe they're from . . .
THE WISE GUY (taking the box from her hands): Flowers for you? You're out of your mind. You're dreaming . . . As a matter of fact, they could be for me . . . wait a minute . . . there's something written . . . hard to read . . . Oh, it says Antoine Doinel! It's for Doinel, how do you like that? Congratulations, old man!

Everyone laughs as he hands the box of flowers to Antoine.

HYDRAULIC PLANT HALLWAY. INTERIOR. LATE
AFTERNOON.
Antoine, the box of flowers in his hands, is waiting for the
elevator. Just as he's about to dump them furtively in the waste-
basket, the manager comes up to him. Both of them step into the
elevator, with Antoine still carrying the flowers.

ANTOINE: What floor?
MANAGER: Ground floor.
ANTOINE: Ground floor.

The doors to the elevator slide closed.

BUILDING COURTYARD. EXTERIOR. EVENING.
Before going up the stairs Antoine tosses the flowers into the
garbage can, but they fall to one side. Little Christophe appears
behind Antoine and picks them up.

DOINEL STAIRCASE. INTERIOR. EVENING.
Antoine, on his way up, is unaware that Christophe is following him with the box of flowers.

DOINEL APARTMENT. INTERIOR. EVENING.
Christine is playing her violin as Antoine walks in.

ANTOINE: Hello.
CHRISTINE: Hello, Antoine. How are things?
ANTOINE: All right.

There is a knock at the door.

CHRISTINE: What's that? Was someone with you?
ANTOINE: No, no one . . .

She opens the door. Christophe hands her the box of flowers.

CHRISTINE: Good evening, Christophe.
CHRISTOPHE: Good evening.
CHRISTINE: What's this?

Christophe shrugs that he doesn't know.

CHRISTOPHE: Can I play with Alphonse, please?
CHRISTINE: Yes. He's in there.

Christophe walks over to the next room. The camera remains on him and Alphonse as the dialogue between Antoine and Christine is heard off.

CHRISTINE (off): Look at what he brought.
ANTOINE (off): I know about them; I brought them for you, but I must have lost them on the stairs . . . besides, I thought it would look silly . . .
CHRISTINE (off): Not at all. I'm delighted. You'd better change your clothes. We're going out this evening. You didn't forget, did you?
ANTOINE (off): I haven't forgotten, but I've got to go back to work. We're testing tonight . . . all night long.

RESTAURANT. INTERIOR. EVENING.
Antoine gently puts his finger on Kyoko's nose.

ANTOINE: And what's this?

KYOKO: Nose? *Hana.*

ANTOINE: *Ana.*

KYOKO: *Hana!*

ANTOINE: *Hana.* When you answer the phone, you say "Machi, machi." What does it mean?

KYOKO: Not "Machi, machi," it's "Mochi, mochi." It means "Hello!"

ANTOINE: That's how you say "hello"?

KYOKO: Yes.

ANTOINE: Well then, if you say "Hello, hello," do you say "Mochi, mochi, mochi, mochi"?

KYOKO: No, just "Mochi, mochi!" [*They smile at each other and she puts her head on his shoulder.*] This is nice, isn't it? You know, if I ever commit suicide with someone . . . I'd like it to be with you.

Antoine is a little taken aback.

A close-up of a miniature Japanese garden. The tiny flowers and plants sway back and forth under the impact of a storm wind. A clap of thunder is heard.

DOINEL APARTMENT. INTERIOR. EVENING.

Alphonse is in his high chair, being fed by Christine. A slight sound from the next room attracts their attention. As the vase of tulips begins to unfold, Kyoko's little messages fall on the table. We hear Kyoko's voice: "Her name is Kyoko—she loves you."

DOINEL APARTMENT. INTERIOR. EVENING.

Antoine, coming through the door, looks back toward the landing, where the tenor's wife can be heard.

SYLVANA (off): I'm coming, here I am . . .

He closes the door and sees that the room inside has undergone a complete transformation. Everything is arranged in pseudo-Japanese style, including Christine herself, who is wearing an Oriental kimono and has two long knitting needles sticking out of her hair, pulled up in a lustrous bun.

ANTOINE: Christine . . .

As she lifts her face to him, her eyes are brimming with tears.

DOINEL BEDROOM. INTERIOR. EVENING.

A little later on. Antoine is trying to reason with Christine.

ANTOINE: If she were just another woman, it would be natural for you to be jealous. But she's not . . . Kyoko is another world . . . a different continent . . . do you see what I mean?

Christine appears, all dressed to go out. She puts her violin case on the bed.

CHRISTINE: No.
ANTOINE (pointing to the violin case): What's that?
CHRISTINE: I'm going to give a lesson.
ANTOINE: At this time? [He opens the case.] What's this? Where is the violin?

We now see that she has packed some clothing items in the violin case.

CHRISTINE: I'm going to spend the night in a hotel. I'll come by for Alphonse in the morning.
ANTOINE: Look, we can both stay here. I'll sleep in the chair and you can sleep in bed.
CHRISTINE (angrily): I won't sleep in the same room with you!
ANTOINE: Oh, if that's the way you want it . . . [Now, he too is angry. He violently heaves the bedclothes onto the floor and hauls the mattress into the next room.] . . . we won't sleep in the same room!

HYDRAULIC PLANT. EXTERIOR. DAY.

A long shot of the basin. The sky is clouded over and a clap of thunder is heard in the distance.

DOINEL APARTMENT. INTERIOR. EVENING.

The dining room is filled with smoke and is rather messy. Antoine, surrounded by sheets of paper, is lying on the mattress on the floor, writing.

The door opens. Christine walks in, with the baby in her arms.

CHRISTINE: Good evening.
ANTOINE: Hello.
CHRISTINE: What a mess. You left without waking me this morning.
ANTOINE: Do you mind if I kiss Alphonse?
CHRISTINE: We were supposed to have a talk this morning.
ANTOINE (*kissing the baby*): Hello, Alphonse.
CHRISTINE: Did you forget?

As she moves off with the baby, Antoine continues to speak very loudly so that she can hear him in the next room.

ANTOINE: Talk . . . there's always time to talk! Besides, I was late for work . . . By the way, your parents called to say they're coming over for dinner. They're on their way.
CHRISTINE (*coming back into his room*): My parents!
ANTOINE: They'll be here any minute.
CHRISTINE: Couldn't you tell them not to?
ANTOINE: I didn't say anything. What could I tell them?
CHRISTINE: You're out of your mind, Antoine. I haven't told Mother about us. [*She hands him the phone.*] Go on, call the garage and say we can't make it this evening.
ANTOINE: It's too late. They called just as they were about to leave the garage. In any case, they'll figure it out when they see all this . . .
CHRISTINE: You're disgusting, really disgusting. When she sees all this, my mother'll feel terrible. Come on, give me a hand!
ANTOINE: Do we have to put everything back in place?
CHRISTINE: Help me.

They haul the mattress over to the bedroom; Antoine's papers fall all over the floor.

ANTOINE: Watch it . . . my manuscript . . . A lot you care about my manuscript!

Later on the apartment is back to normal. The doorbell rings. Christine opens the door to let her parents in.

MME. DARBON: Hello, darling. How are you?
CHRISTINE: Fine.
DARBON: Hello, Christine. Everything okay?
MME. DARBON: We invited ourselves. Did Antoine tell you? [*She hands Antoine some packages she's brought.*] Here's the food. Hello, Antoine, how're you? I want to see Alphonse.
DARBON: Hello, Antoine. How are you?
ANTOINE: Fine.
CHRISTINE (*noticing a yellow toy in Darbon's hand*): What's that?
DARBON: A duck, a little duck for Alphonse.

Christine follows her mother into Alphonse's room; Darbon and Antoine cross the dining room to join the ladies.

DARBON: You seem upset.
ANTOINE: No, I'm fine.
DARBON: Is anything wrong?
ANTOINE: No, everything's all right.
DARBON: Say, the duck isn't for you; it's for Alphonse. You see, I just read a pretty good book, *The Mischievous Duck*. It's the story of a judge, a member of the high bourgeoisie, who falls in love with his son's toy duck. It's very strange.
In the background the two women are huddled over Alphonse's crib, but Christine turns back to answer Darbon.

BED AND BOARD 299

CHRISTINE: You can be sure that won't happen to Antoine. He loves people, not things . . . although he's very partial to yellow.
MME. DARBON (*with the baby in her arms*): Just look at how sweet he is.
DARBON: He's very cute.
MME. DARBON: He's really handsome.
CHRISTINE: He's grown, hasn't he?
MME. DARBON: Yes, he's gorgeous.
CHRISTINE (*to the baby*): Look at the duck!
MME. DARBON: D'you want to go with Mamma?
CHRISTINE: Come to mamma. Look at him stand up. He wants to walk. Watch!

As Christine tries to help Alphonse walk, we see the baby and the legs of the adults; their commentary is heard off.

MME. DARBON (*off*): Christine . . . he's too young!
CHRISTINE (*off*): Go on, Alphonse, go on baby.
DARBON (*off*): He is not amused!

FOYER OF THE DOINEL APARTMENT. INTERIOR.
EVENING.
The door to the landing is opened; Antoine and Christine are partially concealed behind it as they make their farewells to the parents who are already outside.

CHRISTINE: I'll call you.
MME. DARBON: Good . . . in the afternoon. We'll run over to the clinic to see Colette.
CHRISTINE: Good-bye, Lucien.
DARBON: Good-bye, Antoine.
ANTOINE: Good-bye, Lucien.
DARBON: Good-bye.

CHRISTINE: I'm sorry about tonight. I am awfully tired.
DARBON: We were all in bad shape, but never mind. Good night, kids.
MME. DARBON: Go inside . . . you'll catch cold.

Christine closes the door; Antoine, leaning against the wall, lights a cigarette.

CHRISTINE: Help me move the mattress back.
ANTOINE: Look . . . is it absolutely necessary?
CHRISTINE: Yes, it is.

She heads for the bedroom, followed by Antoine.

ANTOINE: Listen . . . the world's not going to come to an end if I sleep next to you. I mean it!
CHRISTINE: I'm not like you. I hate what is vague . . . elusive . . . I hate the ambiguous. I like what is clear-cut.
ANTOINE: Christine . . .
CHRISTINE: Don't come near me . . . don't touch me . . . there is nothing between us.
ANTOINE: Then I wonder what the hell I'm doing here!
CHRISTINE: So do I.

Now Antoine flies into a rage. He dashes into the bedroom, puts his coat on angrily, grabs a bag and throws some of his clothes into it.

ANTOINE: Okay, if that's the way you want it, I'm splitting!

Christine steps aside to let Antoine pass. We hear the door being slammed and the sound of his footsteps running down the stairs.

Christine disappears in the kitchen for a moment, then comes out with a chocolate bar in her hand. She goes over to the door and stands leaning against it, munching the chocolate, her eyes filled with tears.

PLACE CLICHY. EXTERIOR. DAY.
A building next to the Gaumont-Palace with a "Hotel" sign on the facade. A window opens and Antoine appears at the balcony.

DOINEL BEDROOM. INTERIOR. EVENING.
Christine, carrying Alphonse in her arms, goes over to a framed picture of Antoine. She removes it from the frame and replaces it by a portrait of Nureyev.
A title flashes across the screen: "TUESDAY."

KYOKO'S APARTMENT. INTERIOR. EVENING.
Kyoko and Antoine are dining Japanese-style. Kyoko, seen from the rear, is serving Antoine some rice. Facing the camera, he is kneeling on the other side of the low table and smiling.
A title flashes across the screen: "THURSDAY."

The two are having another Japanese meal. Antoine, shifting

around in an attempt to find a comfortable position, looks a little unhappy.

A title flashes across the screen: "SATURDAY."

Yet another Japanese meal. Antoine, awkwardly shifting his legs under him and then straight ahead, seems desperately uncomfortable.

HYDRAULIC PLANT. INTERIOR. EVENING.

Antoine and Monique are waiting for the elevator.

ANTOINE: I don't know what I'm going to do, or how to reorganize my life.

MONIQUE: For the time being, you're by yourself?
ANTOINE: Well . . . more or less.
MONIQUE: Does it bother you . . . being alone?
ANTOINE: I don't mind solitude.

They get into the elevator.

MONIQUE: When I'm alone at night, I'm scared. I'd even marry a lamppost . . . if it could talk!

DOINEL LANDING. INTERIOR. EVENING.
Christine steps out of her door and sees Sylvana.

CHRISTINE: Oh, it's you . . . I thought it was Antoine . . . he was here yesterday, so . . .
SYLVANA: Trust my experience. He'll come back, believe me.
CHRISTINE: I don't think so; I handled it very badly. Instead of smoothing things over, I panicked and made them worse.
SYLVANA: It takes patience. All men are children.

CAFETERIA. INTERIOR. DAY.
Monique and Antoine are seated at a table.

MONIQUE: I thought you were in love with your wife.
ANTOINE: Very much so. At first, I couldn't get over her good manners. She was so polite that it was funny . . . even touching. After a while, it got on my nerves: Thank you for this, thank you for that, thanks for stopping by, thanks for this wonderful meal, thank you for calling . . . God . . . When we were first married, I used to call her "Peggy Proper." "Peggy," because of her Anglo-Saxon reserve, and "Proper," because that's just what she was. Know what I mean?

DOINEL LANDING. INTERIOR. EVENING.

CHRISTINE: When we met, I was a virgin. Mind you, I'm not proud of it . . . on the contrary! My parents gave me lots of freedom, I dated as much as I wanted, but I was scared of boys and I had principles . . . Imagine! A virgin at twenty! I was a living anachronism, a real idiot!

SYLVANA: I had false ideas about life, too. Even so, it's fascinating.

CHRISTINE: No, the truth is that life is disgusting!

CAFETERIA. INTERIOR. DAY.

ANTOINE: I wish you could see her smoking a cigarette. She doesn't know how. She holds the cigarette between her fingers . . . like this . . . like a clumsy little girl acting grown up!

DOINEL LANDING. INTERIOR. EVENING.

CHRISTINE: It's true that he's really funny, and despite everything he's done, I'm never bored with him. He's always got a cold . . . have you noticed? [Sylvana laughs.] At first, when he sniffled, I was irritated. I felt like saying: "Why don't you blow your nose?" But now, when I don't hear him sniffling, I think he's sick.

SYLVANA: There . . . you see? [There is a sound of footsteps on the stairs.] That's my husband. Good-bye.

CHRISTINE: Good-bye, Sylvana.

Both women go back to their respective apartments.

SUBWAY STATION. EXTERIOR. DAY.

Antoine's attention is attracted to a man who is behaving very strangely: It is M. Hulot taking the subway. Antoine goes into the subway car too.

DOINEL APARTMENT. INTERIOR. EVENING.

Antoine has come by to see Alphonse. The doorbell rings. Antoine puts the baby down and goes over to the door to let Christine in.

CHRISTINE: Good evening, Antoine.
ANTOINE: Good evening, Christine.
CHRISTINE: How are you?
ANTOINE: All right—and you?
CHRISTINE: Fine. Was Alphonse a good boy?
ANTOINE: Very. You know, he smiles . . . and he blows kisses . . .
CHRISTINE: You noticed, huh?
ANTOINE: Yes.
CHRISTINE: And did you notice his tooth? It happened the day before yesterday.
ANTOINE: You've got your first tooth, Alphonse.
CHRISTINE: Yes.
ANTOINE: Day before yesterday?

Christine goes over to Antoine with a suitcase in her hand. She has changed her dress; the zipper in the back is still open.

CHRISTINE: I packed your summer clothes for you.
ANTOINE: I'll get them some other time.
CHRISTINE: All right. Look, can you zip me up. I'm late . . .
ANTOINE: Sure. [*He zips up her dress and then leans over the baby's playpen.*] Alphonse is playing with a program. Is it all right?
CHRISTINE: No, he'll tear it up. I went to the ballet a few nights ago.
ANTOINE (*examining the program*): What's written on it?
CHRISTINE: That's Nureyev's autograph. After the show we went backstage to his dressing room.
ANTOINE: That's so provincial . . . bothering a guy who's danced for two hours . . . honestly . . .

The doorbell rings. On her way to the door, Christine answers Antoine.

CHRISTINE: Now, don't start that! [*Opening the door.*] Good evening, Madame Martin.
MME. MARTIN: Good evening. I'm here to baby-sit.
CHRISTINE: Come on in.
MME. MARTIN (*as she sees Antoine*): Am I too early? I can come back a little later, if you want.
ANTOINE: Not at all. Good evening, Madame Martin.
MME. MARTIN: Good evening.
ANTOINE: How are you?
MME. MARTIN: Fine, thanks.
CHRISTINE: Go on in and take a look at Alphonse.

As Mme. Martin heads for Alphonse's room, Antoine whispers to Christine.

ANTOINE: What's Madame Martin doing here?
CHRISTINE: Madame Martin?
ANTOINE: Yes. What's she doing here?
CHRISTINE: She's going to take care of Alphonse. [*Christine picks up the phone and dials a number.*] Hello! Could you send a cab please . . . 17 Rue Descazes . . . In six minutes! Fine, thank you.
ANTOINE: Are you going out?
CHRISTINE: Yes, I am. But you can stay with Alphonse, if you like. Madame Martin can fix you some dinner.
ANTOINE: No, I'll walk you down.

Christine and Antoine go into the next room, where Mme. Martin is playing with Alphonse.

CHRISTINE: Good-bye, darling. Be good.
ANTOINE: Good-bye, Alphonse.
CHRISTINE: Good night, madame.

Antoine gives a final kiss to the baby while Christine puts her coat on.

CHRISTINE (*to Mme. Martin*): You know how to work the television?
MME. MARTIN: Yes, thanks.
ANTOINE: Good night, Alphonse.

In the dining room Christine takes a small painting off the wall and hands it to Antoine.

CHRISTINE: Here, take this Balthus.
ANTOINE: I gave it to you. It's yours.
CHRISTINE: You can have it back.
ANTOINE: Look, it's yours! I gave it to you.
CHRISTINE: Oh, all right then.

She hangs it back and picks up the keys on top of the television.

CHRISTINE (*as they're going out of the flat*): D'you remember how, when we'd go out, you used to say: "I'll take my keys too . . . in case we have a fight." [*She laughs.*]

BUILDING STAIRCASE. INTERIOR. EVENING.
Antoine and Christine are going down.

ANTOINE: It's nice to see you in such a good mood.
CHRISTINE: Does it surprise you? I know that whenever you come here, you're nervous in advance: "She's going to give me hell again." That's what you think, isn't it?
ANTOINE: It's not so!
CHRISTINE: Admit it!
ANTOINE: Certainly not.

He kisses Christine; she pulls away.

CHRISTINE: You mustn't kiss me.
ANTOINE: Oh? I thought . . .
CHRISTINE: No.
ANTOINE: Well, I just thought . . .

BUILDING COURTYARD. EXTERIOR. NIGHT.
As they get to the courtyard, Antoine takes Christine's arm. She shakes him off.

CHRISTINE: Let me go!
ANTOINE: I was just helping . . .
CHRISTINE: I don't need any help!

Antoine steps away from Christine and leans against the wall of his former workshop.

ANTOINE: You're very unpleasant tonight, really very unpleasant.
CHRISTINE: And you're irresponsible! All you know is what you want: I'm supposed to kiss you when you feel like it . . . to leave you alone when you want to think . . . I'm not "yours to command!"
ANTOINE: All right.
CHRISTINE: Not anymore!
ANTOINE: That's enough! [He moves over to her.] Look, I'm sorry . . . I understand how you feel . . .
CHRISTINE: Oh, I know that line: "I understand you . . . I'm a bastard . . . you're much too good for me!"
ANTOINE: I don't pull that.
CHRISTINE: You've done it a hundred times. You can put it all in your novel . . .
ANTOINE: As a matter of fact, it's almost finished. It's all I can

think about right now. That's why I'm so fouled up. But I'm sure that once it's done, we'll get along better.

Antoine kisses Christine again and this time she lets him. Then she heads for the doorway, as he follows, a few steps behind.

CHRISTINE: Don't send me a copy. I won't read it. I don't like the idea of telling all about your youth, of blaming your parents, of washing dirty linen in public . . . I'm not an intellectual, but I know this: writing a book to settle old scores isn't art!

Moved by Christine's sincerity, Antoine stops walking and looks down.

ANTOINE: As a matter of fact, I've been wondering about that . . . that's what's bothering me.
CHRISTINE: Do what you must, but leave me alone. I haven't got much pride; I've never had, so I can tell you that I still love you . . . But I'd rather not see you anymore. From now on, let me know when you come to see the baby, so that I won't be home. Come on, the cab's on its way.

STREET. EXTERIOR. NIGHT.
Christine is outside on the sidewalk, as Antoine closes the door behind them.

ANTOINE: Where's that cab?
CHRISTINE: They said it would take them six minutes . . . What about you? I hope you're happy.
ANTOINE: I don't even think about it. It's hopeless . . . even now we can't think of anything to talk about when we're together.
CHRISTINE: You can always smile at each other.
ANTOINE: That's all we do. By evening [*he grasps his jaw and*

presses it in his hand] I've got lockjaw from smiling so much. But the worst is in the restaurants . . . between courses. She smiles and waits for me to make small talk. I can't even eat. It's really awful. I got myself off the hook by telling her I'd be out of town for three days.

CHRISTINE (*laughing*): I feel sorry for you. [*The cab pulls up in front of them.*] Here it is. Where are you going?

ANTOINE: I don't know.

CHRISTINE: Can I drop you off?

ANTOINE: No, I'm okay.

CHRISTINE (to the driver): Just a minute! [To Antoine.] I can cancel my date and stay with you. We could go to the movies, if you like.

ANTOINE: No, I prefer to be by myself . . . I'll just go for a walk. You're sweet . . .

CHRISTINE (from inside the cab): Kiss me.

Antoine leans over and kisses her gently, caressing her face.

ANTOINE: You are my kid sister, my daughter, my mother . . .

CHRISTINE: I'd hoped to be your wife.

The cab rolls off. Antoine walks slowly along the street.

ANOTHER STREET. EXTERIOR. NIGHT.

Antoine arrives in front of a building, the door of which is lit up. He checks the street number and walks in.

BUILDING STAIRWAY. INTERIOR. EVENING.

A young woman in a red dress is walking up ahead of Antoine. At the landing, the woman opens the door and indicates to Antoine that he's to go in.

YOUNG WOMAN: Wait here. I'll be right back. [She leaves the room.]

In a little while a dozen girls come down the stairs from the floor above. They go into the room where Antoine is waiting and form a circle around him. Antoine, flustered, tries to run out, but he is stopped by the young woman in red, who is presumably the manageress.

MANAGERESS: Where are you going? Don't you like any of them?
ANTOINE: I didn't know it was like this . . . I'm a little embarrassed.
MANAGERESS: It's very simple. You take a look, you pick one out, and then . . . you know . . . go on!

She pushes Antoine back into the room. Clearly ill at ease, he looks at the group, then points to one of the girls. She is tall, quite beautiful and has long, dark hair. With the manageress leading the way, she and Antoine leave the room as the girls start up the stairs again.

PLACE PIGALLE. EXTERIOR. NIGHT.
A long shot of the Place Pigalle, brightly illuminated by a multitude of neon signs.

HOTEL ROOM. INTERIOR. EVENING.
Marie, the girl Antoine has picked out, is putting her clothes on again.

MARIE: It's sort of slow right now. We used to be busy till the twenty-third of each month. Now, everyone's broke by the fifteenth. Some administration! The minute I saw what they looked like on TV, I knew we'd had it. Aren't you interested in politics?
ANTOINE: A little . . . But I agree with you: they're all bums!
MARIE (combing her hair): Yeah. Some bums cost us more than others. And remember: "If you don't follow politics, politics will get you in the end." Especially at the end of the month!
ANTOINE: The end of the month, the end to an end . . . I hate everything that comes to an end, I hate all endings [muttering to himself] . . . it's the end of the film . . .

MARIE (*on her way to the door, stops*): What's that?

ANTOINE: Nothing. I said that you are beautiful, Marie . . . especially beautiful.

He kisses her hand and walks downstairs as she stands there, looking at him.

HOTEL STAIRWAY. INTERIOR. EVENING.
A few steps down, he turns back to Marie.

ANTOINE: Good-bye.

As he proceeds downstairs, he hears someone coming up; he stands aside to avoid the man, but it is too late. Behind the manageress, who is leading the way, is his father-in-law.

DARBON: Well, Antoine! You look as if you're walking in your sleep. I'm glad to see you. [*Darbon cordially puts his hand on Antoine's shoulder.*] There's nothing like a good house to complete a happy home!

M. Darbon continues to follow the manageress up the stairs, while Antoine runs down and out.

PLACE CLICHY. EXTERIOR. DAY.
A long shot of a corner of Place Clichy. In the background, the Gaumont-Palace and next to it the hotel where Antoine lives. Antoine is crossing the street, weaving his way through the traffic. As he reaches the sidewalk, the moocher walks up to him.

THE MOOCHER: Hi, there! I owe you one hundred, right?
ANTOINE: Me? No!

Antoine dashes off. The moocher seems rather baffled as he watches him go.

BUTTE MONTMARTRE. EXTERIOR. DAY.

The title superimposed on a long shot of the Sacré-Coeur, reads: "THREE DAYS LATER."

DOINEL APARTMENT. INTERIOR. EVENING.

Christine is playing with the baby. When the phone rings she puts Alphonse in his crib and goes over to pick it up.

CHRISTINE: Hello.
ANTOINE (off): Christine?
CHRISTINE: Yes.
ANTOINE (off): It's Antoine.
CHRISTINE: How are you? Where are you?

PHONE BOOTH IN A RESTAURANT. INTERIOR.
EVENING.
ANTOINE: I'm okay. I'm in a restaurant.
CHRISTINE (off): And . . . ?
ANTOINE: And nothing . . . nothing special. I just felt like talking to you. I've got to go.

DOINEL APARTMENT.
CHRISTINE: Wait. Anything wrong?
ANTOINE (off): No. It's just that . . . I'm not alone . . . I'm with someone.

RESTAURANT.
CHRISTINE (off): Mademoiselle Butterfly?

ANTOINE: Right. I just can't take it. She never says a word. She just keeps smiling. She expects me to be funny, to tell her jokes. I'm sick of it, really fed up. I'm not even trying . . . to hell with her!

DOINEL APARTMENT.
CHRISTINE: Antoine, there's no point in being nasty.
ANTOINE (off): All right. Anyway, it was good talking to you. So long.

RESTAURANT.
CHRISTINE (off): Good-bye.
ANTOINE: Good-bye.

Antoine hangs up the receiver, goes out of the glass phone booth, walks down a few steps and across the room to a table at which Kyoko is seated.

KYOKO: Did you make your call?
ANTOINE: Yes.
KYOKO: Good.
ANTOINE: Why did you wait? You should have started.

On the plates in front of them is the meat course. Quick cut of the restaurant clock. We go back to the plates, which are now empty. Antoine knocks his knife against the plate to attract the waiter's attention.

WAITER: Finished?
ANTOINE: What's next?
WAITER: Certainly. Would you like some cheese?
ANTOINE: No thanks! Oh, sorry, Kyoko . . .
KYOKO: Yes.

ANTOINE: Let's have some cheese!
WAITER: I'll bring the tray over. [*He walks off.*]
ANTOINE: Excuse me, Kyoko. I've got to make another call.
KYOKO: Yes.
ANTOINE: I'm sorry.

He gets up and crosses the restaurant again, heading for the phone booth. A quick cut to the restaurant clock shows that it is getting late. Inside the booth Antoine has already dialed the number.

CHRISTINE (*off*): Hello?
ANTOINE: Hello, Christine. It's me again.
CHRISTINE (*off*): Still at the restaurant?
ANTOINE: Yes. It's just as I expected . . . deadly!
CHRISTINE (*off*): Well, I hope the food's good.
ANTOINE: Rump steaks! In total silence! Each minute counts triple! It feels like I've been here all day long.
CHRISTINE (*off*): Try to talk to her.
ANTOINE: Impossible! I'm bored stiff. I just want to beat it. After the meat, she ordered some cheese! Okay, I've got to get back . . . but if she orders dessert, I'll kill myself!

Antoine hangs up the receiver, goes down the steps and across the restaurant. Kyoko now has a plate of cheese in front of her.

KYOKO: Are you sure you don't want any cheese?
ANTOINE: No, thanks.
KYOKO: This one's very good.

As she eats her cheese, Antoine keeps on looking at the phone booth, which is being used by another customer. One of the waiters glances at his watch to check the time. The people at the table behind Kyoko and Antoine have left and their table is being cleared.

ANTOINE: Excuse me, Kyoko. Another phone call.
KYOKO: Yes.

Antoine crosses the restaurant, which is now almost empty. At the steps leading to the phone booth he intercepts a waiter who's carrying two cups of coffee on a tray.

ANTOINE: Are those for us?
WAITER: Not yet. Yours will be served after dessert.
ANTOINE: Oh! Well then, bring us the check with the coffee.
WAITER: Very well.
ANTOINE: Remember: At the same time!
WAITER: Yes, sir.

Antoine goes into the phone booth. A quick cut to the clock hands shows it is getting very late.

DOINEL APARTMENT.
Christine lifts the receiver off the hook.

ANTOINE (off): Christine, hello. It's me again . . .

RESTAURANT.
Back to Antoine in the phone booth.

ANTOINE: She simply doesn't understand. She's just ordered a soufflé . . . that'll take at least twenty minutes . . . [A pause.] Are you there?
CHRISTINE (off): I'm here . . .
ANTOINE: Say something.

DOINEL APARTMENT.
CHRISTINE: I'm listening.

ANTOINE (off): You know . . .
CHRISTINE: I'm listening.
ANTOINE (off): I can't talk from here. I'd like to kiss you.
CHRISTINE: Me too.
ANTOINE (off): Tenderly.
CHRISTINE: Me too.
ANTOINE (off): Is that true?
CHRISTINE: Yes, it's true.

RESTAURANT.
ANTOINE: Good-bye.

The clock hands indicate that it's now close to midnight. Antoine crosses the restaurant. Midway he looks ahead and seems
surprised. We follow him to the table. Kyoko has vanished. The
table has been cleared away; only two glasses remain. Kyoko has left
a little note between them. Antoine picks it up. The message is
written in Japanese, but the subtitle reads: "DROP DEAD!"
    A fade-out is followed by the title: "EPILOGUE—ONE
YEAR LATER."

DOINEL LANDING. INTERIOR. DAY.
    The door to the Doinel apartment is open. Antoine is pacing
up and down the landing, continually checking the time on his
watch.

ANTOINE: Come on, come on.

A child's rubber toy rolls out of the door, stopping at his feet.
Little Alphonse, who has grown since we last saw him, runs over
to the toy. Antoine lifts him up and kisses him.

ANTOINE: Say "Papa—Papa." Go back inside.

He puts the child down and gently smacks his bottom as he leads him to the door. Inside we catch a glimpse of Christine running by.

CHRISTINE: I'm coming!

Antoine goes back to his pacing and time-checking. After a while he goes into the apartment, to emerge a few minutes later with Christine's fur coat and purse. After throwing them down the stairs, he starts to go down himself. Christine now appears in the door and throws an aggravated look in the direction where her coat and purse have disappeared.

BUILDING STAIRCASE. INTERIOR. DAY.
On his way down, Antoine passes the opera singer and his wife going upstairs. We follow them up until they find Christine's fur coat and purse. Christine now comes down. Sylvana and her husband help her get into the coat.

CHRISTINE: Thank you. I'm very late. Thank you very much. [She hurries down the stairs.]

The singer and his wife lean over the banister. As the sound of Christine's footsteps grows fainter, Sylvana turns to her husband.

SYLVANA: You see, dear. They're truly in love, now.

The singer glares at his wife. The image freezes on his irritated look.